An Angel Among Us

An Angel Among Us

Lee Springgate

ISBN: 1500360546
ISBN 13: 9781500360542

Table of Contents

Introduction

*There are two ways of spreading the light; to be the candle or
the mirror that reflects it.*

— EDITH WHARTON

A very special young man needs a witness to his life. Scott, our
thirty-four year old son, was born three months before the erup-
tion of Mount St. Helens. We should have seen it coming. He can't
speak, read, write or effectively communicate his thoughts, experiences
and feelings. Scott's story is an intimate journey into the depth and
breadth of a profound developmental disability. His life is a testimonial
to unconditional love. At his very core he exudes a purity of spirit,
untarnished, undeniable and unassailable. Truly, what you see is what
you get. He has no personal agenda. He has no intrinsic need to ma-
nipulate others to achieve power, control, status, recognition, wealth or
attention.

His needs are acute, but so are his assets. He has an innate ability to
draw people into his world, with a penetrating gaze, bear hug and infec-
tious laugh. We feel blessed to catch fleeting and intermittent glimpses
of God's love. The unconditional love creates the glue that protects the
individual and strengthens the resolve, empathy and commitment of the

family. The world of a profound developmental disability is a confounding, heartbreaking, and enlightening place, one inhabited by a fraction of humanity. It's a lifetime journey, one that doesn't end until "death do us part." This unspoken vow is infinitely stronger than that proclaimed so visibly by married couples the world over.

You don't just walk away from it at the first sign of strife or discomfort. A powerful bond cements this vow, which demands a life of sacrifice, struggle, acceptance and adjustment. It's a game changer in every sense of the word, a trip filled with mountains and valleys, sunshine and darkness. The challenges, at times, are overwhelming and accompanied by unrelenting guilt. Through it all, you have the the certain knowledge that you are needed and that your loved one has value and a special place in the universe. Our son speaks through us to leave a lasting and unique footprint in a world desperately in need of love, acceptance and compassion.

Despite the enormous challenges associated with his care, there resides within this very special person a God given ability to love and be loved. He has a pure spirit that radiates love and innocence. His soul, to borrow from an Al Pacino character, is in-tact and we are all richer for being in his orbit.

Every human being, even the most profoundly disabled, has the capacity to make a contribution to the world in some fashion. This story describes Scott and his family's journey through the bewildering and perplexing world of developmental disabilities. It's a story worth telling and long overdue, but can it ever really be conveyed and understood?

Is it too far removed from normal everyday experience to really matter to the vast majority of people? Will families struggling with a difficult diagnosis find in valuable? Or, will it ultimately undermine the fragile support network needed to sustain the acutely vulnerable person? Can too much information conveyed too early sow seeds of doubt, hopelessness and futility? Is it best to allow bonds to cement, families to adjust and hope to thrive?

In the final analysis, ours is a very personal story of one family's thirty-four year experience with a profound disability. We trust that more good than harm will come from telling this story and we believe that truth and love will ultimately prevail over false expectations and self-deception. We don't pretend to represent any family other than our own, but we suspect that our experience is shared, to a large extent, by other families' coping with physical and cognitive disabilities.

We write this story for a number of reasons. First, we hope to give voice to our own non-verbal son who has virtually no avenue of complex communication available to him. He cannot talk, sign, write, read or convey thoughts, needs or ideas through pictures or symbols. Although we obviously can't relay his most fundamental thoughts and emotions, we can offer observations from our front- row seat to this lifelong drama.

Second, we want our extended family to better understand what's transpired over these past thirty- four years. One of our great regrets is that we could not participate effectively in normal family activities, from Christmas and Thanksgiving gatherings to birthdays, graduations and weddings. By necessity, we've been isolated and cast adrift, but we neither accept nor assign blame. As they say, "it is what it is."

Third, we want this story to be read and understood by future caregivers and guardians who will inherit the day- to- day responsibility for our very special son when the inevitable aging process escorts us from center stage. We want caring and sensitive people to value him, in a realistic context. It's our final dream and prayer for our son.

Fourth, we hope that other families in an earlier phase of caring for a profoundly disabled person will find this story to be of some value. We've navigated through some very stormy times and we hope that our experience will help others cope and prevail.

Finally, in the event that professionals, from neurologists and pediatricians to educators and therapists, actually take the time to read about a story told from a parent's perspective, we hope to offer a modicum of enlightenment.

It's been a life- altering journey, but one we were clearly meant to take.

The Prelude

God grant me the serenity to accept things I cannot change,
the courage to change things I can, and the
wisdom to know the difference.

— REINHOLD NIEBUHR

You probably are familiar with the old adage "If you want to make God laugh, tell him your plans." My wife, Jean, and I were the quintessential young professional couple prepared to share our life and wisdom with children who were given up for adoption. Surely nurture would soundly trump nature and we would put our indelible stamp on this child and guide him or her to a successful, independent life.

I would like to say that this was an easy, comfortable decision for both of us, but that simply wouldn't be the truth. I didn't initially embrace adoption, or, for that matter, having children at all. My mother had a severe heart attack at age thirty-six that, in retrospect, was accompanied by a degree of brain damage and personality change. She lost the ability to care for her children and this placed a traumatic strain on the entire family. I was introduced at the tender age of fourteen to the realities of caring for young children. The Brady Bunch had left town, leaving a broken shell of a family. The point of this little diversion is that I had a pretty realistic view of how challenging and difficult it is to properly raise and guide a child in this increasingly complex world.

Jean and I had been married for thirteen years. We each had satisfying professional careers and had an extraordinary degree of freedom and independence. Jean, nevertheless, desperately wanted a family and we made a valiant effort to conceive. Extensive fertility treatments were still relatively new and prohibitively expensive and, frankly, I was quite content with living our "childless" life. I wanted to go ahead and make our contribution through our professions and volunteer work and fully enjoy our carefree lives. As we came to this fork in the road, I was perfectly content with staying the course and living the good life.

However, this approach was definitely comparable to swimming upstream in a society that clearly expected young married couples to procreate and pass on their precious DNA to generations of children and grandchildren.

Despite the seismic societal shifts of the 1960s and 1970s, "married with children" was still the norm, a suffocating expectation. Of course there were childless couples, but, certainly, they didn't choose their barren life. Surely, some external condition, from infertility to disability to illness, conspired to rob the loving couple of their cherished dream.

Quite candidly, I have always been plagued by an underlying pessimism about humanity and its capacity to survive its own acute limitations and foibles. Greed, selfishness, religious fanaticism, resource scarcity, proclivity to violence, environmental degradation, and a host of other issues have always suggested to me that the human race is on the precipice.

Jean, a superb first- and second- grade teacher, with a strong maternal instinct, was intensely driven to have children and, if we could not have our own, she wanted to adopt. Since I was reluctant to bring a child into this turbulent world anyway, I concluded that it would do no harm to adopt. Although ambivalent about the entire idea of parenting, I understood that Jean would not feel fulfilled otherwise, and there was a distinct possibility that it would lend greater meaning to my own life.

As excited as Jean was to adopt a child, she did give me one final chance to opt out. I quote, "if you think adopting a child will change our life in any way, we shouldn't do this." Failing to visualize how adopting a child could put a major dent in our lifestyle, I assured her I was ready. We blissfully plunged into the deep end of the pool without a second thought. To this day, we still chuckle over our cluelessness.

An opportunity presented itself in late 1979 when Jean's sister put us in touch with the wife of a private physician caring for a young woman who planned to give her child up for adoption. After some preliminary conversations, we were asked to visit the physician at his home in Bremerton Washington, apparently to confirm that we had our shots and could be trusted with this immense responsibility. Jean was so nervous on the hour-long ferry ride from Seattle to Bremerton that it was touch and go as to whether she would get through this ordeal. But the interview was congenial and the physician gave us his blessing to proceed.

After hiring an adoption attorney and filling out interminable paper work from King County, we waited on pins and needles for the birth to take place and on August 4, 1980, we were informed that the mother had delivered a very healthy and robust baby boy. They were very pleased to let us know that he had a perfect score on the Abgar scale, a test administered to newborns at the time to assure that all the vital signs were normal.

The final agonizing part of the adoption process involved waiting for three days after birth to ensure that the biological mother didn't have a change of heart and crush our parental dreams. Having cleared this hurdle, we were given the green light to pick up our new born boy from Harrison Memorial Hospital in Bremerton. Packing the Buick with all the baby paraphernalia and intrusive in-laws, we took the ferry to Bremerton on a sweltering ninety- degree day to start a harrowing thirty –four- year journey into a parallel universe.

The nurses in the maternal unit greeted us and expressed great relief that parents had finally arrived to take their precious charge to a loving home. The delivery doctor, who just happened to have one of the biggest noses we've ever seen on a human being, arrived soon thereafter to give us a briefing. Jean, in one of those really great ironic moments, took her first look at Scott, looked up to the doctor and asked whether he thought Scott's nose was too big. So our most pressing concerns at the beginning were that Scott might have a big nose and be small in stature because of the height of the birth parents. In retrospect, it's just amazing what we get exercised over and what we take for granted.

In the interest of full disclosure, no, we had no idea that Scott would have a disability of any kind. It was the furthest thing from our mind and had we known in advance of his birth, I'm sure we would have opted out of the adoption. This is probably the first question people ask us after they learn that Scott was adopted. It's an interesting question because we don't know whether people find it more surprising or virtuous that people would make the decision to adopt a disabled child or to keep a disabled child that they had not anticipated. Either way, it's a life- altering decision, one guaranteed to have a profound impact on the way you view the world.

A Normal Interlude

For a blissfully short time, prior to our indoctrination into the twilight zone, we led the lives of normal parents of a newborn child. Sure, our lives were altered by the lack of sleep, loss of freedom, paranoia over health issues, and the steep learning curve associated with caring for a newborn. But this was just normal stuff that all rookie parents encountered.

Like everyone else, we were able to take solace in the fact that "this too would pass". We would gradually recover our bearings and rejoice in watching our child reach all the highly anticipated milestones—first step, first word, first day of school, soccer, T- ball, sleepovers, school performances, first date, school graduations, first day of college, first job, marriage, children. The sky's the limit, anything's possible. We were excited to provide the guidance and support necessary for Scott to achieve his dreams and aspirations. Everything would unfold as it should, and we were anxious to see how his life would evolve and what kind of mark he would leave on the world.

It's a heady time to be a parent. All options are on the table and you believe with all your heart and soul that your child will lead a happy and constructive life. Your job as a parent is to provide structure, stability, wisdom and support and get out of the way as your child carves out the life he or she is meant to live.

Parenting transforms you, leaving you a different but improved person, ready to take responsibility for the well-being of a fragile, vulnerable life. Obviously, it's not the only way to make an important and meaningful contribution to the world, but it does have a tendency to take you by the shoulders and steer you toward a more purposeful existence.

So we were in that contented state, where everything was normal and anything was possible. We blew through the first six months, experiencing our first Christmas together as an expanded family, attending family functions and getting acclimated to our role as first- time parents.

It was also a time when we bonded with our son. I've learned through the adoption process that bonding is not the exclusive domain of biological parents. I view it as a kind of spiritual umbilical cord, proof that all things in the universe are connected in some bizarre fashion. We made a very intense connection, almost instantaneously, and it provided Scott with a form of divine protection and intervention. It also gave his parents their first glimpse of unconditional love, that capacity to love another person without demanding anything in return. It was probably Scott's greatest gift to his father particularly, a startling reminder to live a service-centered life.

The Diagnosis

We can't help everyone, but everyone can help someone.

— Ronald Reagan

As a new parent, how do you every really know when something's amiss? We had no immediate diagnosis, missing body parts or other telltale signs to provide any kind of early warning. Everything looked just fine to our naïve eyes and we had no reason to suspect that trouble was lurking in paradise.

Gradually, much like the lobster in the pot, it began to dawn on us that something was not quite right. After about seven months, doubt started to penetrate our carefully crafted Hallmark life when we noticed that certain developmental steps were lagging. Scott had a pronounced head lag and he wasn't beginning to crawl, climb or babble. Since infants and toddlers develop at different rates at this tender age, we were inclined to write off the discrepancies. Just to be sure, Jean scheduled an appointment with his pediatrician to do a quick evaluation and provide the necessary assurance that everything was just fine.

It was at this point that the first bucket of ice cold water was poured over our heads. Anyone who has ever encountered a serious medical issue knows that it's never a good sign when your gateway doctor recommends that you see a specialist. You know the line, "it's probably nothing serious, but let's just double check with the specialist to make sure." Scott's developmental progress did not fall within normal parameters, so it was time to bring in the first team.

So we dutifully made an appointment, and the day finally arrived when the man in the white coat would officially declare that our son was safely perched in the middle of the bell- shaped curve. Our blood pressure could return to normal, and our fears would be laid to rest.

Observing the sacred medical practice of arriving twenty minutes late for the appointment, without so much as an "I'm sorry" or a reassuring smile, word or gesture, the doctor started his clinical evaluation. In perhaps the most astonishing medical examination we've ever encountered, he turned Scott upside down to test his airplane reflex, turned to us and said he had cerebral palsy. He recommended that we immediately go to the lower level of the hospital and schedule a series of appointments for physical therapy.

That was it. We didn't have the slightest idea what cerebral palsy was or how it would affect our son's life. We didn't receive written or verbal information about this diagnosis, just ushered out of the office and given directions on how to find the physical therapy clinic.

The diagnosis was shocking, confusing and debilitating. We were stunned, unable to process our feelings. In a matter of moments, we were teleported from the normal world to one euphemistically described as "special." While we didn't really know it at the time, our life would never be the same. It was like two plates of the earth's crust crashing together and creating a volcanic upheaval. Nothing looked or felt the same again and we became engaged in a battle for emotional survival.

We felt blindsided, angry at the universe and uncertain about what to do next. This was pre Internet, so we had to dig and plead for relevant information about the diagnosis. About all we were told was that cerebral palsy is a brain injury that occurs just prior to, during or immediately after birth. The injury could be physical, mental or a combination of the two. It could be mild, moderate or severe. Anytime we requested more specificity we were told that only time would tell. We just needed to get Scott to therapy immediately, a legion of specialists would do their magic and the severity of the brain injury would be revealed. Just have faith in the experts, provide a loving family support system and all would become clear in due time.

So that's how it was supposed to work? Stand aside and let the professional take control of our lives and his future? We were quite naturally terrified by the prospects. We have all seen people with various forms of cerebral palsy, the spastic, involuntary movement of limbs and head or a rigidity that requires use of a wheelchair. While their minds might be perfectly normal, their physical impairments guarantee a life of major challenges. If they have both mental and physical injuries, they will probably require extensive caregiving support for the balance of their lives. It's a sobering prospect, one far, far beyond anything we envisioned as parents.

The therapists were absolutely adamant that early intervention could go a long way toward healing or ameliorating the initial brain injury. The idea was to establish alternative neural networks that could bypass the injured parts of the brain and allow Scott to do those things he otherwise would be unable to do. Time was of the essence and intensive intervention needed to occur while the brain was most pliable. This plasticity is a characteristic of developing brains and alternative networks needed to be created before the brain started its inevitable pruning process. Excess neurons are shed as the brain matures and, theoretically, our developmental path becomes more defined and inflexible.

So we were in a race against time, but we, as parents, were not allowed to participate in the race. We were reasonably successful professionals and the idea of being a passive spectators to our son's fate didn't sit particularly well. By God, we were going to defeat this disability through sheer hard work and fierce determination. We were not going to walk away from this fight. We were needed and we had a track record of success in our life. Scott deserved our relentless advocacy and we wouldn't let him down. He was loved unconditionally and we had a sacred obligation to see that he was given every opportunity to develop to his full potential.

This was our feisty mindset as we settled into our role as parent advocate. Let's be honest here, we were not the least bit prepared to accept defeat. We were not Mother Teresa walking the slums of Calcutta administering to the poor and infirm. We were not going to accept the disability, plain and simple. We would face the challenge head on, come out victorious, and get on with our normal lives. If, in the end, Scott had to accommodate a mild physical disability, so be it, but it would not materially affect his ability to lead an otherwise normal life.

Nothing in our prior lives prepared us, spiritually or emotionally, to accept permanent responsibility for a developmentally disabled person with profound mental and physical challenges. If anything, I was probably the poster boy for insensitivity and callousness when it came to interacting with the physically and developmentally disabled. It's hard to admit that I was not a choir boy ready and willing to offer a lifetime of love and support for a profoundly disabled person. To be honest, this is probably the last thing in the world I envisioned for my adult life. Sainthood clearly was not in my DNA. I wasn't out there looking for an opportunity to give and sacrifice: the opportunity found me when I wasn't looking.

My early behavior toward the physically or mentally challenged was, to say the least, deplorable. While I'm not proud of the following examples, they do serve to illustrate how a life can be transformed by unconditional love. Sometimes, the very object of ridicule and ignorance becomes the source of personal enlightenment.

I remember walking in downtown Seattle with a good friend while we were in our teens. We passed a group of adult men who appeared to have some form of spastic cerebral palsy. They had a substantial amount of involuntary movement in their arms, hands and head and that naturally drew the attention of two smartass teenagers. As soon as they passed, my friend, going for the cheap laugh, broke ahead of me, mimicked their walk and involuntary arm and head movement and pretended to eat an ice cream cone that missed the mark and crashed into his forehead. I, of course, thought this was the funniest thing imaginable and broke out in hysterical laughter. People passing by me thought that I was laughing at a disabled person and gave me the stink eye, but it didn't really faze me. We had a good laugh at the expense of people who had to endure significant challenges every day of their lives. Like everyone else, they just wanted to be accepted and allowed to lead as normal a life as possible.

I vividly remember sitting on the bench while my Franklin High School baseball team was at bat during a game with West Seattle High. Sitting next to me was the same friend who amused me so much with the cerebral palsy group. The first baseman for West Seattle was a young man who had lost his leg and was courageously playing with an artificial limb. Well, rather than showing this guy the respect he so richly deserved, my buddy started cracking a series of jokes that had all his juvenile buddies, including me, in stitches. "Hey, this is the only guy I know that can dive into the water and come up feet first.-When this guy wants to bunt, he just lifts his leg. When he slides into home plate, he yells timber." On and on it went for nine innings, a relentless assault on an amazing young man by a bunch of immature goons.

I remember that our baseball team had a team manager who, in retrospect probably had a mild developmental disability. We, of course, never really accepted any kind of deviation from the norm and proceeded to harass and bully him. Once, we even threw his mitt out the window of the bus and had a good laugh. It's just so hard to believe we could have been this callous and insensitive, but we were. Every member of that baseball team still owes this guy an apology, fifty years later. Yes, times were different and prejudice flourished against minorities, gays and the disabled, but it was never justified under any circumstance.

Finally, fast-forward seventeen years and I was in my first years as director of the City of Bellevue's Parks and Recreation Department. I was visiting one of our park sites where two Special Olympics teams were playing a softball game. Apparently, after failing to evolve emotionally or spiritually from my high school years, I couldn't stop laughing after watching a fly ball fall between three outfielders. Yes, their hand- eye coordination was less than optimum, but they were trying, having fun and getting the most out of their ability. That was far more than could be said for me at the time.

These examples just confirm how unlikely a candidate I was to raise and support an adopted, developmentally disabled son. Candidly, Jean and I were seduced into accepting this responsibility by a deep, almost irrational, love of a vulnerable child and the fervent belief that we could overcome the disability. A divine intervention was at play that protected our son, while simultaneously drawing us deeper and deeper into a lifetime commitment. Honestly, it's hard to imagine, had we known the extent of his disability when we embarked on this journey, that we would have embraced the long- term responsibility and sacrifice. We approached the fork in the road with trepidation, without any idea that our new destination wasn't even on the map.

So after absorbing the initial diagnostic shock, we set our sights on conquering the mountain top. It was time to roll up our sleeves and attack this threat to our son and family. For the next eighteen months, we followed the lead of our professional guides, the therapists, pediatricians and neurologists. Initially, Jean drove a half hour each way to take Scott to physical therapy at Group Health Cooperative twice a week. Taking their cue from the rest of the medical community, the therapists would frequently arrive late and finish early, running him through a series of exercises designed to improve weight bearing, balance and coordination. Jean's role was to get Scott to the appointments, provide strong parental support and follow through in any manner they thought was appropriate.

Rather than striving for a true partnership between the parents and the medical team, a very strong bias was in play that favored a separation of roles. The professionals would take responsibility for his developmental progress and the parents would provide the loving, supporting home environment. They wanted us to just let go and allow them to do what they were trained to do and accept whatever conclusions they reached. His developmental progress was in their hands, so just needed to relax and keep the home fires burning.

It wasn't as though his therapists were disinterested or incompetent. They were generally very kind, sympathetic and supportive. It was very easy to just succumb to their hypnotic spell—to relinquish personal responsibility for his development to this community of experts. They repeatedly assured that Scott appeared to be bright eyed, alert and fully capable of making amazing developmental progress. This soothing reinforcement, while well intentioned, has a tendency to lure you into complacency. You have a tendency to take your eye off the target when you believe that the experts are hitting the bull's eye.

After a few months of this physical therapy regimen, we had a follow-up appointment with our pediatric neurologist. After conducting a follow up examination that included measuring Scott's head size, evaluating his cognitive development and testing his reflexes, he informed us that Scott would probably be "mildly retarded." He hoped that Scott would one day be able to walk, talk, and get accepted into a sheltered workshop.

Once again, we were stunned and immobilized by this shattering diagnosis. We meekly left the doctor's office and drove for a while in a collective daze. We pulled over at a turnout that had a panoramic view of Lake Union, looked at each other and wondered whether we could continue along this path. Should we pull the cord and bail out? This wasn't what we bargained for when we adopted this boy, so was it time to relinquish the responsibility to the state or another family more capable of handling the situation?

But after taking a long, hard look at our son, I told Jean that this boy needed us, and she readily agreed. We were all in, our chips were on the table, and we were going to play this hand to its conclusion. But we were not going to do so passively. This show would no longer be directed exclusively by the professionals, we were going to be exacting and active participants. To put it bluntly, we were not prepared to accept the diagnosis.

This child was placed in our care for a reason and we would not let him down. Whatever it took to influence and redirect the wiring in that evolving brain would become our mission. God help anyone or any bureaucratic system that stood in the way of this goal. He would not be deprived of his chance at a normal life and we would make whatever changes we needed to make in our lives to reach this objective. We were not going to be accused, in retrospect, of failing him at this crucial time in his life simply because we were too unimaginative, undisciplined or complacent. We were ready to roll up our sleeves and slay the dragon.

This was our breakaway moment. We decided to turn our back on a system that was inherently omniscient and paternal, one that directed us to a hierarchy of experts who would concoct a therapeutic cocktail designed to modify and mask the brain injury. We chose not to be passive spectators who would allow our lives to be directed by a small army of professionals who, in the final analysis, were unaccountable for the results.

A number of months pass and Scott was still not showing any measurable progress. He wasn't crawling, standing, walking, speaking, playing with toys or interacting normally with other people. Doubt permeated our minds and we began to question the validity of what we were being told. A quiet desperation emerged as we realized that we were not winning the race. The onus was on us to find the right treatment program or this boys' chance at a normal life would be irretrievably lost. Guilt, the omnipresent companion of every DD parent, burrowed into our consciousness. It never left our side. It kept whispering in our ears that we should do more, advocate more effectively, work harder and make better decisions. Scott's future was in our hands. We had a moral obligation to do anything and everything in our power to help him survive and thrive.

Frustration built as progress remained stagnant. Soothing assurances from professional therapists started to sound hallow and unconvincing. We located a birth- to- three center close to home that had a growing reputation for making significant progress with infants and toddlers diagnosed with a variety of developmental disabilities. Jean made the decision to double down, taking Scott to therapy twice a week at Group Health and twice a week to the birth- to- three center. It was an arduous process, one hour to get him ready, forty minutes travel time each way and one hour of therapy, four times a week. Presumably two different institutions working twice as much on his therapeutic needs should result in significant and noticeable progress.

While therapists gleefully pointed out small examples of progress, something still didn't feel right. First, why weren't parents being educated on the therapeutic techniques and enlisted to augment his program at home? Were the exercises so complex and technical that they were beyond the capability of motivated parents? Second, how could four hours a week of hands-on therapy really achieve substantial results? Wouldn't a more intensive intervention stand a greater chance of success in creating the new neural pathways? Third, was the limited amount of direct therapy from professionals worth the tradeoff in time and energy required to get Scott to his appointments four times a week?

We were convinced that intense, creative intervention would yield immediate results. It would be comparable to providing CPR to a drowning victim, a child's future would be resuscitated by our heroic efforts. Relying on our own life experiences, we were persuaded that a little old- fashion faith, elbow grease and creativity would tilt the odds in favor of our son. He would come out of the other end of the intervention tunnel a changed child, a success story for the ages. We would unsaddle our white horses, take a bow and get on with the business of living.

> *Never believe that a few caring people can't change the world. For, indeed, that's all who ever have.*

— MARGARET MEAD

The Messiah

About this time, we came in contact with the charismatic founder of a national organization devoted to working with developmentally disabled children. This organization practiced a maverick approach that advocated an intimate partnership between parents and professionals. Accepting an invitation to attend a lecture by this young dynamo, we were captured and mesmerized by his message of hope and the necessity of intense, focused and direct parental involvement. His mantra of "frequency, intensity and duration of appropriate stimulation" struck a responsive chord and for the first time in our lives we became disciples.

His message was simple and entirely believable. If we only worked hard enough and followed his enlightened direction, dramatic progress could be made in Scott's development. Our son's brain was just injured and injuries can heal with appropriate treatment. Hope was alive, and we were reenergized and willing to commit wholeheartedly to this radical departure from the classic therapeutic model.

He proselytized, to be sure, but his message resonated with parents plagued by doubt and helplessness. Were they doing enough for their children, and should they continue to concede the initiative to a cadre of paraprofessionals who worked on an appointment basis a few hours a week? This condescending approached failed the sniff test for the more aggressive and demanding parents. Wouldn't it make more sense to have these experts empower parents to work directly with their children many, many more hours a week? Would just a few hours a week of therapy *really* make that much difference and why wasn't more progress evident from the existing regimen?

So when a charismatic, intelligent and persuasive missionary for the "brain injured" arrived in our beleaguered life, we were ready to follow his lead. To repeat his message, first, the parents were the real experts in their child's life. Second, frequency, intensity and duration of stimulation could make dramatic progress in healing the brain injury. Third, parents could be trained to provide that stimulation. Fourth, the parents could train volunteers to assist in delivering this augmented program.

All it would take to "heal" our brain injured son was faith in the organization's philosophy and a Slavic devotion to hard work. Scott's progression from developmentally disabled to normal was entirely up to us. The program's approach disdained labels that put our children in self- prophesized boxes, like mentally retarded, Down syndrome, cerebral palsy and attention deficit disorder. "Don't let anyone tell you what your child is capable of becoming: there are no limits to his or her development." Well, that message was certainly music to the ears of parents wallowing in self-pity and despair. After receiving discouraging long- range developmental forecasts and being shuffled to the background by a tone - deaf medical establishment, along came a brash, confident, arrogant messiah. Move out of the way you guardians of the status quo; there is a new sheriff in town.

What a powerful message of hope, a rope thrown to a couple of parents wallowing in quick sand. His appearance in our life quite possibly preserved our sanity and gave us new direction and motivation. On the reverse side of the equation, when hope is revived and responsibility placed squarely on your shoulders, guilt replaces despair as your principle antagonist—a kind of devils bargain. It would be our fault now if he fails to make any progress. As we all know, life presents a complex web of tradeoffs and we would need to be ready to accept a compromised personal and family life if we accepted this challenge. The classic teeter- totter metaphor applied; the more weight we would give to work and family, the more we would shortchange his long term development. However we chose to balance the two, something would give and a load of guilt would accompany our choice.

The program was an all-consuming, merciless companion that dominated our family life for the better part of five years. We made the hard decision to work directly with our son. How else could we ever look in the mirror years later and say with absolute conviction that we did everything we could? We didn't choose expediency or conjure up some sophisticated rationalization that he would be better off left in the care of professionals or placed in an institution. He deserved our best efforts and that's what he would get.

So what did this program look like? How did it operate? Who was this guy? Was he legitimate? Did the program deliver the promised results? Had we momentarily put on some rose colored lenses in our frantic search for answers?

He and his staff would provide a program for parents to implement, and he would see us every three months to measure progress and provide an updated program. At the time, his organization was headquartered in California. He established chapters in a number of western states, including Washington State, and he passed through the area every three months conducting seminars and evaluating clients. For DD parents starved for hope and inspiration, he was our version of Billy Graham, always positive, hopeful and insightful.

The various chapters were run and managed by parent volunteers. They would organize seminars, secure evaluation sites, make hotel reservations, schedule appointments and make regular contact with new parents on the program. It wouldn't be long before Jean assumed responsibility as a chapter co-chair, as if raising two toddlers and providing Scott's home therapy program weren't enough responsibility.

With great anticipation, we awaited our first evaluation just as Scott turned eighteen months. Our new leader spent a good hour evaluating

Scott's developmental progress and appeared quite optimistic about his prospects. The programs that he prescribed were geared specifically to individual clients. He provided an imaginative and very time consuming set of exercises designed to stimulate alternative neural networks. As a general rule, it took about five hours a day to complete the prescribed program and we repeated specific program elements three or four times per day.

We placed a plastic mask over his mouth and nose twenty times a day for two minutes to push additional oxygen into his lungs. We played audio tapes repeatedly to encourage language development. We provided tactile stimulation to his fingers, toes and mouth four times daily. We placed peanut butter on the roof of his mouth to stimulate his tongue. We assisted him physically to cross- pattern crawl, a precursor to standing, climbing and walking. We built a device that stabilized his feet and allowed him to stand against a wall and do knee bends four times a day. We built a special overhead ladder that allowed him to walk under it, holding on to the railings above his head.

To assist her with this daunting assignment, Jean recruited a group of volunteers. We created posters that we plastered at various churches and shopping areas and put out an SOS to friends and family. Eventually, as many as thirteen volunteers came into the house weekly for as much as five hours a day, providing much- needed physical and psychological support. It was incredibly disruptive and chaotic, but it had to be done if we stood any chance of success.

As an interesting aside, most of our volunteers came from the Catholic Church. We are not Catholic, but we greatly admire their service ethic and remain eternally grateful for their support during this turbulent time. A special thank you to my sister, Kathy, a converted Catholic, for taking time out from raising her own three children to come across the county to volunteer with Scott. We were at that stage where we found it difficult to put the full- court press on for support from family and friends. We were probably just a bit too proud and independent to freely admit how much we needed help from those closest to us.

Sometimes, false pride can be your own worst enemy. For the sake of your loved one, make your needs clear. It's unreasonable to expect everyone to read between the lines and provide whatever it is you require at the time. After all, this is the essence of family and friendship, to be there for one another during times of crises.

It's easy to be seduced by the right message and the right messenger. Our ability to critically evaluate the message was clouded by our underlying desperation. Make no mistake about it, when you see your child slowly, inexorably sliding out of the mainstream, you grab for any lifeline. We had already come to the conclusion that his current therapy programs were ineffective and that we needed to take a more active role in his development. The program's message was extraordinarily timely and we were ready to shed our usual skepticism and wrap our arms around its iconoclastic leader. We had this underlying feeling that the sand was running out of the hourglass and he just might be able to halt Scott's slide into an irreversible, lifelong developmental disability.

Talk about a sense of urgency! Everything depended on this moment. As long as there was a glimmer of hope, we felt that we had no choice other than to do anything and everything you could to coax him into our "normal" world. The alternative was just too hard to imagine, too painful to accept. We had to push with everything in our arsenal while there was still a battle to win, and our champion appeared just in the nick of time.

Interestingly, his appearance in our life occurred almost simultaneously with the adoption of our second child, Stephanie. So just as we are prepared to embark on an intensive home therapy program for Scott, along came the demands of a newborn, catapulting Jean into a parental frenzy. This dual responsibility was amazingly difficult, a real drain on her energy and sanity, and a tribute to her dedication and tenacity. This was in addition to taking Scott twice a week to his appointments at the birth to three center. To this day, I don't know how she survived.

So, we put our faith in "the Man", slipped on our track shoes and began the race of our lives. It's hard to describe the schizophrenic nature of our lives at this time. On the one hand, we were trying to lead a normal family life. We would go to the park, take rides, visit the zoo, ride the ferry, go to movies and eat out. We would take the kids to visit Santa Claus, attend Easter egg hunts, go trick or treating and attend Fourth of July concerts. We would vacation to Maui, Yellowstone, Disneyland and the Oregon Coast.

We were determined to look and act like a perfectly normal family. We wanted Scott to experience as many normal activities as other children, even though he had to endure this relentless therapeutic badgering from well-meaning family and volunteers. He was entitled to a childhood. All therapy and no play would be lopsided and counterproductive. He needed some semblance of balance in his life, and his parents needed a break from therapeutic jail. It helped that Scott was a very good- looking child, easy to transport and assimilate into a wide variety of settings.

We were able to project a normal image to the outside world, a bit of deliberate deception. Remember, from our perspective, Scott's developmental delay was a temporary problem that our enlightened intervention would remedy in a relatively short period of time. In the meantime, we were determined that Scott would not be prematurely labeled and pigeonholed. He would lead a normal life while simultaneously being subjected to an intense barrage of home therapy.

But, of course, just how normal was this life, for us or Scott? We were frazzled from the demands of working, caring for young children, running a house, managing volunteers, overseeing the local home therapy branch, taking Scott to traditional therapy appointments and implementing the program.

Scott, bless his young soul, was bombarded by family and volunteers with a bewildering array of funky exercises. People were always manhandling him, moving him from one exercise to another, trying to bypass the injured parts of the brain. He was always being pushed, prodded, cajoled and manipulated. Through all this harassment, he maintained a surprisingly good disposition, the consummate good trooper.

This was not what any of us imagined would be the life of an eighteen-month-old toddler. What a strange way to experience life's first stage for both Scott and his parents. It was a baffling, infuriating detour, but we would be back on the road to normal in no time.

The Surprise From Left Field

*The pessimist complains about the wind; the optimist expects
it to change; the realist adjusts the sails.*

— William Arthur Ward

Just as we settled into this bipolar routine, Scott started experiencing
a debilitating seizure disorder. He had micro seizures, when he would
briefly lose consciousness, lose his balance and drop his head. He was
experiencing up to one thousand seizures a day. He was virtually out of
commission for the entire day, unable to function and at risk for personal
injury. Lord knows what these seizures were doing to his brain and its capacity to process new information and perform its basic functions.

This was a crises of the first order. We raced to his neurologist and
pleaded for relief. This poor kid would lift his head momentarily and immediately experience another seizure. His life was on hold until the doctor
could find a medication or combination of medications that could work on
this threat to his life and our sanity. For several months, we experimented
with a variety of medications, all to no avail. It was a very, very depressing
time in our lives. Everything was totally out of our control and he wasn't
getting any better. Nothing we experienced before or since could compare
to this sense of hopelessness and despair.

With no relief in sight, we experimented with the ketogenic diet. This
was a diet that had been around since the 1930's used as a last resort for

seizure disorders. Although it had a decent track record of success in treating out of control seizure disorders, it had fallen out of favor in later years as anticonvulsive medications made their appearance on the market. The basic premise of this diet is that carbohydrates have to be dramatically reduced and replaced by fat and protein. Carbohydrates produce glucose that most of us use to fuel our brain activity, but too much glucose can be a major contributor to epilepsy. Increased fat induces the liver to produce ketogens that can replace glucose as a source of fuel for the brain.

The diet was difficult to prepare, and Scott detested the heavy dose of fat and protein. He's always been a carbohydrate guy, and he wasn't the least bit pleased with the change. But Jean diligently prepared his special meals and coaxed him to eat what he obviously hated. After several months of this diet, it was clear that his seizures were not influenced by the change. We remained in limbo.

During this time, Scott had what we thought was a major epileptic seizure. His arms and legs were shaking and he essentially lost consciousness. We called Medic One and rode with him to the hospital in a state of panic. It turned out that he had a febrile seizure, which was not all that uncommon in young children. While relieved that his seizure disorder had not graduated to a life threatening level, we were still despondent over his condition.

We would be remiss if we didn't mention how impressed we were by the Medic One personnel. They were calm, assuring and competent. His life was obviously in good hands and we are thankful that they were there for us on that dreary day.

The seizure disorder continued unabated until the doctor decided to have him admitted to the hospital for several days of observation. The hope was that the medical staff could try additional medications and keep a close eye on him while they experimented with various combinations.

We celebrated our thirteenth wedding anniversary at the bedside of our extraordinarily fragile son, praying for a miracle. After the third day, the doctor hit upon a magic combination of medications that dramatically reduced the magnitude and severity of the seizures. Thirty- two years later we are still administering the same two medications three times a day and other than times when he's extremely tired or ill, the seizures are under control.

Seizure management requires constant vigilance. Regular blood draws are needed to measure whether he is at the proper level, therapeutic, but not toxic. If you lose your focus and forget to administer the drugs or give him the wrong dose, you run the risk of triggering another unmanageable episode or, conversely, turning him into a lethargic zombie. His chance to lead a reasonably happy life depends on the ongoing control of this under-lying seizure disorder.

Seizures are just one significant example of the life and death respon-sibility that parents and caregivers inherit when they accept responsibility for a profoundly disabled person. In Scott's case, he has always needed to be within hearing or sight. He has never had any inherent sense of danger and he would walk right into traffic or walk off the end of the dock or over a cliff if something attracted his attention. He still can't be left unattended in the bathtub or a swimming pool. He indiscriminately approaches people who visually interest him. You need to take his hand as he descends stairs or slopes or he will trip and fall. Leave him unat-tended next to a hot stove and would likely get severely burned. There is no room for error: one misstep and he winds up in the hospital or, God forbid, dead. You don't get the day off because you are tired, sick or in-capacitated in any way. Forget about indulging a midlife crises or taking time to "find myself." Eternal diligence has been a mandatory require-ment for thirty- four years and will be until the baton is passed to his next generation of caregivers.

Coping with a developmental disability during its earliest stages is a bit like purgatory. You are not in hell, but you are far removed from the Promised Land. Grief is elongated and distorted. You don't know precisely what you are grieving over, other than your child is not currently normal and may never be part of the mainstream. Over time, as the condition gradually reveals itself to you, grief reemerges like a wound that won't heal. You are riding this emotional roller coaster, alternating between hope and despair. Grief always resides just below the surface, ready to suck you under like a riptide. It doesn't recede with time: it just resurfaces with the gentlest provocation.

This crushing responsibility reshapes your personality and perception of the world at large. Metaphorically, you are under house arrest, tethered to your son and his staggering array of needs. So much of what we observed on a daily basis appeared superfluous. People appeared, at times, to live easy lives, unencumbered by serious matters. Self-absorption struck us as a wasted opportunity to live a meaningful life, yet, paradoxically, we envied the freedom, flexibility and spontaneity that accompanied this lifestyle. The point is that we were irrevocably changed, forever attentive to the needs of another human being. While we wistfully watched others lead more normal lives, we accepted the bargain that we had made with God. We were needed for more important things than riding around in a golf cart, climbing mountains or traveling the world.

We retained our sense of humor and enjoyed the life we had been assigned, but if the truth were told, this caregiving was a deadly serious matter that required our constant attention. As we move through this fourth decade of living in the DD world, we are more and more persuaded that we were meant to live this life. Besides, there is no worse preoccupation than comparing oneself with others. Everyone has something of significance to deal with in life and the only thing that really matters is how well we respond to the challenge we've been given. The comparison game is a dead-end proposition. First, appearances are deceptive. There are always those who appear to be doing better than us, but how do you really know what is going on in their life? Secondly, there are hordes of people struggling every bit as much or more than us to make it in this world. We are not alone: life is full of challenges and hardship. We need to check our self-pity at the door, embrace life and focus on making this a better world.

The Home Therapy Years

The next five years of Scott's life were dominated by this amped up version of home schooling. Volunteers rotated in and out of his life, and he continued to undergo hours and hours of therapeutic intervention. Jean, trying to cover her bet, continued to take him to the birth- to- three center for the first couple of years. He "graduated" from this program at age three with a rather unceremonious send off. Those same therapists who thought he showed such great promise at one time confided to us that he was not the "star" that they thought he would become. This was our first introduction to the one- way accountability street. If things went well, they basked in his reflected success. If not, they washed their hands and accepted absolutely no responsibility. It was always his problem, his failure, his responsibility.

This pattern was repeated time and time again throughout his school years. We deferred to the trained experts, they designed and implemented the intervention program and periodically reported back to us that he'd failed to reach any targeted goals. The most exasperating part of this circus is that they never made any midcourse corrections. They just keep herding our kid along to the next year without measureable progress and expected us to thank them profusely for their sainted work.

The normal progression for developmentally disabled kids at age three is to be passed along to the school district for inclusion into their early intervention program. Theoretically, the birth-to-three centers have done a sterling job of intervening during the formative years and it's time to enroll their little success stories into the school system. With detached bemusement, we read all these stories about how incredibly important birth- to- three centers were to a child's development. This cutting- edge intervention was supposed to be a lifesaver for countless numbers of developmentally delayed children. Their deficits would be addressed during this critical time in their development and they would be far better prepared to enter school and prosper alongside their normally developing peers.

We can't speak for other children and their families, but, in our case, the birth to three center made very little headway with his development. We couldn't detect any significant progress over the two and a half years that we was placed in this program. It was almost as though we never enrolled him in the first place. He obviously wasn't ready to be "graduated" to the public school system. The whole experience with the birth to three program was very disappointing and completely inconsistent with their external hype and image.

We presume that their program achieves results with a certain number of DD children, but they failed with regard to Scott. It wasn't the last time that a program failed to achieve results after leading us to believe that it had the secret formula. If results were achieved, the program took total credit. If it failed to achieve its goals and objectives, it placed the responsibility squarely on the shoulders of the child. It was dishonest and disingenuous and an all too common occurrence.

Our advice to any parents following in our footsteps is to ride herd on the therapists at this critical time, particularly if you are not seeing results. Demand that they try different approaches and exercise some creativity. If they are not achieving agreed-upon objectives, expect them to be honest. You know Einstein's definition of insanity---doing the same things over and over and expecting different results. Stop doing that which doesn't work, your child deserves better! If everyone is doing everything possible to treat your child and progress is negligible, then, so be it. It's probably a fairly clear indication that your child is headed toward the "special" life, a life that will rock your world.

So at the conclusion of the birth- to- three experience and a year and a half into the home therapy program, Scott still wasn't speaking, standing independently, walking, playing with toys, interacting normally with children or adults or manipulating objects in his environment.

We kept recruiting volunteers, returning every three months to visit the DD whisperer. We got revised program direction and received encouragement and assurances that a breakthrough was just over the horizon. Scott began to stand independently and walk without assistance under the overhead ladder. He learned to cross pattern crawl and climb up the furniture. He looked more curious and alert and we were cautiously optimistic.

Finally, around his fifth birthday, we witnessed our very own miracle. Scott took his first steps and our world lit up like a Christmas tree. What a red- letter day in our life, confirmation at last that he is about to punch through the DD barrier and join the ranks of his normal peers. It was such fun to watch him embrace his new freedom of movement and explore his world independently. He could actually walk from one place to another, without the assistance of another person. Can you imagine how it must have felt for him to make his own choice about when to move and where to go? What was just another normal developmental passage for the vast majority of human beings became a cause of major celebration in our household. Our hard work and dedication had been validated and we once again believed that our young man had untapped potential.

It was so exciting to watch him race around and around the filbert tree in our backyard with such joy and exhilaration. He could now walk in stores, throughout the house, along the sidewalk and in the park. He was like a butterfly shedding his cocoon, a beautiful little boy exploring his big new world.

I couldn't wait to take him to our neurologist, who, until that time, had been a little skeptical about our devotion to the home therapy program. I put Scott against one wall of the examination room and had him walk independently to where I was standing on the opposite wall. The good doctor was astounded and admitted later to me that it brought tears to his eyes because he had been convinced that Scott would never walk.

It was probably the high-water mark in all the years that we spent doing home therapy. We had finally overcome his impenetrable resistance to any and all therapeutic strategies. We sincerely believed that this was just the first of many breakthroughs. It was time to fasten the seat belts and race on to the next series of destinations. Soon, he would be talking, running, jumping, playing with toys, interacting with other children and dressing, toileting, bathing and eating independently.

We were reenergized, ready to continue our battle with the skeptics. But then a funny thing happened on the way to the award ceremony. Scott stopped progressing significantly beyond his mobility advancements. He appeared to hit a developmental plateau and we were absolutely stymied. Had he finally reached his potential? Did we have to reassess our goals? Was it time to recalibrate and accept less ambitious objectives?

This plateau highlighted the critical importance of parent support groups. The hardy band of like-minded mothers who comprised the Washington State chapter of this national organization were Jean's colleagues, confidants and life-long friends. They were coconspirators, committed to doing whatever it took to give their DD children a fighting chance to live a more normal life.

This particular support group was like no other. It cast an inclusive net, inviting anyone under the tent who was dealing with any type of developmental disability. This group didn't limit membership to just Down syndrome, autism, cerebral palsy, or other diagnosis. They were fighting for a common cause. They were battlers, willing to walk the less travelled path and embrace experimental and controversial options. They were not ready to throw in the towel and succumb to a suffocating diagnosis. Their precious charges were not going to be prematurely labeled and pushed into the "special" category. They were not prepared to welcome the little yellow bus up their driveway before it was absolutely necessary. Perhaps that lay in their future, but not before they exhausted every conceivable alternative.

What a relief to know that there were kindred spirts out there who shared our anxiety, fears, hopes and combative spirit. Friends, family, neighbors and co-workers couldn't really know what we were feeling or going through. It was just too far removed from their frame of reference. Empathy was out of their reach and sympathy was unwelcome, so fellow travelers filled the void. It was even difficult to identify with parents of DD children who appeared to be taking the easier, less demanding route. They were cheerleaders of the establishment, less inclined to take chances and challenge the status quo.

The support group was on an island, removed from both the mainstream population and the established DD hierarchy. This isolation strengthened the bonds of friendship between these women who embraced the same cause and approach. They were there for their children, they were there for one another and they were there for the organization. As the organization and its unique therapy model receded into oblivion, their friendship survived and prospered. It was forged by mutual hardship, love and respect. It was a residual, unanticipated benefit of raising a developmentally disabled child, a lifelong blessing.

So take a belated bow, Linda, Lynn, Joan, Marilyn, Jean and the rest of the gang. Your incredible sacrifices on behalf of your children may have been ignored or unappreciated, but that's what made you so special. You have never sought the spotlight or lobbied for sainthood. You were driven by the purest of motives, the well-being of your very special children. As the years marched on and you came to grips with the fact that your children were facing a lifetime of significant challenges, you were always there for your kids and for each other. I salute your tireless dedication, loyalty and spirit!

The Concession

If you do not change direction, you may end up where you are heading.

— Lao Tzu

These home therapy years, so full of hope and promise at the beginning, came to a merciful conclusion when Scott reached about seven years of age. The program didn't live up to its unbridled optimism and Scott was falling farther and farther behind the development curve. It's really very hard to determine just how much all the sacrifice and dedication had achieved. Scott's mobility had, indeed, improved dramatically, but he had made very negligible cognitive progress. He still wasn't speaking or dressing, eating, toileting or bathing independently. He wasn't playing appropriately with toys or interacting normally with other people or his immediate environment. He was developing other challenging tactile behaviors, such as a fascination with water and plastic or placing dirt on cardboard.

The family had reached a threshold. We were collectively burned out, particularly Jean, after a five -year odyssey through this gut-wrenching, unrelenting program. Without a shadow of a doubt, this program preserved our sanity and gave us reason to aspire and hope for a normal life. It gave us a measure of control at a time when we were floundering and rudderless. It gave us precious time to adjust to a reality that was just too hard to accept. It provided structure, shored up our resiliency and instilled in us the confidence to advocate and think independently. We would never again be passive observers, too timid or insecure to challenge authority and conventional wisdom. It gave us the backbone to question, badger, criticize and demand. For all these contributions, we remain grateful to this day.

But, at the same time, the program was a bit of fool's gold. It had all the glitter of the real thing, but failed to deliver on its grandiose promises. It exaggerated its capability and disguised its inherent limitations. The messiah was omniscient, but the disciples were flawed. The program itself was inspired, but the implementation was lacking. Guilt was piled on our shoulders with a bulldozer; any failure to progress was a direct result of our failure to work hard enough. Interestingly enough, it was never presented in this way. It wasn't as though our esteemed leader was taking us to the woodshed every time we appeared at our quarterly evaluations. After all, he needed the quarterly fees that we paid for his wise council and direction and he relied on Jean and the other mothers to keep the chapter afloat. Probably, as a direct consequence of his absolute certainty and confidence, the pressure to work hard and deliver results was omnipresent. Ironically, the sanity that the program initially preserved began to unravel under the unrealistic expectations and disruption to our family life.

As stated earlier, it was our first flirtation with a charismatic healer. We were vulnerable and receptive to his message of hope and healing. At that time in our lives, we needed what he was offering. It's hard to know what would have happened in our lives had we not embraced his message. It was probably a necessary diversion, one that may have given Scott his best chance to live in a loving and supportive home. However, the time, energy, guilt and disruption associated with this program was a price paid by every member of the family.

So we bid adieu to home therapy and prepared ourselves for reentry into the traditional DD delivery system. It was also the time when we reluctantly re-set our goals for Scott. A genuinely normal life for Scott appeared now to be out of reach; it was time to finally accept the inevitable.

It wasn't fair to Scott or the family to keep striving for the impossible. We had to concede his limitations and begin a new quest to make his life as rich and meaningful as humanly possible. We had to continue being his primary advocates and cheerleaders, but we now conceded that his life would never be normal. We still felt the same urgency, but our energy was now directed at getting him the help he needed to achieve a reasonable degree of happiness and independence.

Make no mistake, this was a huge concession on our part. Our fantasy of forcing a square peg into a round hole with sheer willpower had shattered, never to reappear in our lifetime. We put our egos in check and we finally understood that it wasn't within our power to mold Scott into a normal child. We could now relax a bit, accept Scott's limitations and begin a new quest to make him as independent as possible. It was like setting out to climb a sheer rock cliff, establishing finger holds, making some progress and then losing your grip and falling back to earth. The goal was now to find a more manageable peak, ascend by a more conventional route and celebrate each milestone. The summit was probably out of reach, but we could climb as far as possible with the help of some experienced guides.

It was now time to graciously welcome the little yellow bus. We were done protecting Scott with a metaphorical blanket. He was developmentally disabled and we couldn't protect him any longer from the outside world. We couldn't hide the diagnosis; it was out of the closet and we were ready to get on with the rest of our lives.

In retrospect, normal was a seductive and elusive goal, something so important, yet progressively out of reach. As the years passed, the gap widened between what he could do and what he should be doing, both physically and cognitively. From all outside appearances, Scott looked like a normal infant and toddler. He was easy to manage and even drew admiring glances and comments. While we intellectually comprehended the challenges that lay ahead, we indulged our dreams and presented a united front to the world. Eventually, our feverish pursuit of normal yielded to a more relaxed acceptance of a very unique human being.

We became more accepting, less judgmental. As all those pesky milestones went chugging by, like a train, we remained on the platform looking at all the kids and their families moving rapidly out of sight. Earlier in his life, these milestones might have appeared attainable, although just out of reach. Over time, they became a mirage, enticing glimpses of water in an arid desert. Eventually, we shrugged our shoulders, wiped away a tear and soldier on. He was not going to experience anything resembling the life that we knew and he certainly wasn't going to fulfill any of the dreams and expectations we had for his life.

When other parents and their children rejoice in these rights of passage, you hold your son on the sidelines and celebrate their progress. The unrelenting sadness eventually releases its vice like hold on your consciousness. You come to accept that you and yours have your own mission to fulfill, a different life to lead and a special love to share with the world. It becomes time to embrace the unique and special and do everything you can possibly do to make his life as fulfilling and meaningful as possible.

Collateral Damage

The measure of who we are is what we do with what
we have

— VINCE LOMBARDI

A wise person once told me that when one member of the family is disabled, the entire family unit is disabled. This is true on so many different levels, from relationships between spouses (distressingly high divorce rates) to relationships between parents and other children to relationships between extended family and friends. The entire applecart is flipped upside down and the family is left to pick up the pieces and create a new normal.

Life is never the same, no matter how fervently you wish it to be. It just becomes extremely complicated. In the early years, while you still hold out hope that normal is within reach, it's just too painful to watch other kids in the extended family soar past him as they develop normally. He can't interact with other kids, he doesn't play normally with toys, he's not toilet trained, he doesn't speak, he can't walk and his behavior is a little odd. Young children are naturally curious and ask questions. Adults have a wide range of reactions. An ex- brother-in-law once hovered around our eating area during one Christmas Eve gathering with a broom and dustpan to pick up food that Scott spilled on the kitchen floor.

Family gatherings were perilous and stressful. We spent an inordinate amount of time focusing on Scott. It was almost impossible to interact normally with the rest of the family. He was often overwhelmed by all of the stimulation and activity. He needed special help with eating and we had to watch his grabbing and mouthing. We watched silently as he showed more interest in the wrapping paper than the present. He didn't respond in a normal fashion to other family members.

He became restless and agitated and we kept a watchful eye out for toileting accidents. My father's generation, in particular, looked on with a kind of morbid curiosity, unable to fathom why this kid wasn't locked away securely in a state institution. This sentiment, while verbally unexpressed, was painfully apparent. My father never asked about the progress we're making with Scott, whether we were doing O.K or how he could help. He invited my daughter to spend time with he and his wife, but didn't include Scott in the invitation. He never provided a word of support or encouragement and it's clear that he was bewildered by our commitment and sacrifice. I do think this attitude is shared by a very large percentage of the populace, regardless of their generation.

Inexorably, we drifted apart from extended family and retreated into a protective shell. A regrettable casualty of the disability is the opportunity to get to know and interact with nieces and nephews and their families. We became distant relatives, an afterthought in their busy lives. As time passed and we had the opportunity to attend weddings and family reunions, it became very clear that we had paid a dear price for this extended separation. We didn't get to participate in their lives, relate to them in a normal fashion or strengthen family bonds. They, in turn, were not involved in our lives or given the opportunity to know, appreciate or accept our son.

It was a loss all the way around. We missed out on the lives of our siblings, their children and grandchildren and they lose a very special opportunity to know and love a very special and unique human being. His natural support system shrank and he became more dependent upon immediate family and the State Division of Developmental Disabilities.

Caring for a person with profound cognitive and physical disabilities is a daunting responsibility. Everything changes, nothing remains the same. Your life is redefined in an instant and the change lasts a lifetime. Much like the person you are caring for, your family life becomes "special." Birthdays, holidays, reunions and similar family rituals that unite and bind families are sacrificed to protect your loved one and preserve your sanity.

In hindsight, I think we should have tried harder to integrate him into the fabric of the extended family. It would have taken more insight and patience than we were able to muster, but it's a shame that Scott was left on the sidelines. He deserved better and I regret that we didn't have the stamina or determination to make this work and give him the extended family he deserves. Everyone would have been richer for the experience.

The Early School Years

We make a living by what we get, we make a life by what we give.

— WINSTON CHURCHILL

At the time, the Lake Washington School District designated the Gordon Hauck Elementary School to be the primary school for developmentally disabled children three years and older. This segregated educational model separated developmentally disabled children from their normal contemporaries. The staff included special- education teachers, aids and a cadre of physical, occupational, behavioral and speech therapists. No doubt about it, there was a stigma associated with sending your child to this school. Once you entered this special-education bubble, you are branded, corralled and separated. Some kids received very specific remedial help and then sent to regular schools, but the majority were destined to spend their elementary school years in this protected enclave.

While, at first blush, this segregated model might appear to be a bit archaic, it was actually far more enlightened than what existed prior to the passage of special education legislation at both the state and national level. A pioneering group of parents from Seattle instigated this legislation that provided opportunities, for the first time, for developmentally disabled children to receive a public education. Before this legislation passed, the vast majority of DD children were not welcomed within the public school system. They were either warehoused in state- supported institutions or cared for by family members in their home. Many of these children were perfectly capable of learning, but were denied the opportunity simply because they didn't look or act normal. It was yet one more example of blatant discrimination directed at anyone different from the mainstream population.

A segment of society that had been virtually locked away and invisible politely knocked on the door and asked for a seat at the dinner table. It wasn't a dramatic million man march on the Capital or a showdown at Selma. Most of these folks didn't have the capability of developing political strategies, raising money and advocating directly for themselves. Their righteous case was presented passionately and effectively by their family, friends and advocates. It was a noble undertaking that warrants our respect, admiration and appreciation.

At long last, developmentally disabled children were given the opportunity to learn and develop to their full potential. They were no longer written off as a lost cause, incapable of learning and unworthy of our support. Most of us as we were growing up in the 1950s, 1960s and 1970s had little, if any, contact with the developmentally disabled. They stayed out of sight and out of mind, sheltered from the mainstream by protective parents or one of those mysterious state institutions. We couldn't accept what we couldn't understand and we were perfectly happy to keep these special people at an arm's length distance from polite society. It was what I refer to as the deep exclusion model, unenlightened, cruel and indifferent.

So after the moral sledgehammer broke down barriers to a free education, special classrooms and schools mushroomed into existence throughout the United States. Before too long, sheltered workshops, group homes and the Special Olympics made their appearance and it became possible for the developmentally disabled to live, work and play outside the home or institution. It was definitely progress, although it partially mirrored the "separate but equal," doctrine that had applied for so long to the African American community.

As the years have passed, it became the new paradigm is to place all developmentally disabled students and adults in the least restrictive environment. The objective is to eventually integrate this population into regular employment, housing and classrooms. This will be discussed in a later chapter, but we clearly owe a debt to those whose shoulders we stand on today. They achieved heroic goals.

For the first time, Scott was placed in a special-education classroom. His needs and deficits were so acute that we were frightened to let him get on that little bus by himself. How would he be accepted and treated by the teacher, aides and other students? Could he learn anything in this school setting? Would he be safe and respected? Would he behave himself? Since he didn't speak or communicate in any effective manner, how would we really know how he was being treated? How could we know whether they were giving him the support and assistance he needed to learn and progress? We had made this concession to the "system," but was it the right decision?

Anyone who has had the experience of placing their children, for the very first time, in a preschool, kindergarten or first grade setting understands this anxiety to some degree. But to do so with a non-verbal child multiplies the tension tenfold. In addition to our own angst, we agonize over how Scott was perceiving the change. What was he thinking as we put him on a bus with a strange bus driver that would be met at the School by another strange person who, in turn, would take him to a classroom full of strange children and adults? Did he feel confused, frightened, angry or abandoned? We had virtually no way to effectively prepare Scott for this stark change in his life and we prayed that he could adapt and integrate into this home away from home.

It's become a constant obsession with us, trying to see the world from his eyes. Living with Scott has enhanced our empathy, a lasting, irreplaceable gift. We have a greater capacity to walk in someone else's shoes and feel what they are feeling. Not that we can ever truly understand what someone else is going through emotionally as a result of trauma and life circumstances, but, at the very least, our antennas have been enhanced.

Jean, quite naturally, visited the school that first week and learned that Scott had been placed in a classroom with the most profoundly disabled children. She was mortified. She saw no evidence that they were working on anything meaningful. After observing Scott and the other kids from the classroom being walked down the hallway holding onto a rope, her worst fears are confirmed. She was convinced that any progress he'd made to date would be quickly erased by a total lack of stimulation. Expectations would be adjusted and Scott would be riding the elevator all the way to the bottom.

In her inimitable way, she marched down to the Principal's office and demanded that Scott be placed into a different classroom, with a reasonably enlightened teacher. Unwilling to be flattened by Hurricane Jean, the principal agreed to relocate Scott to a classroom led by Sarah Cooper, a dynamo with a natural talent for teaching developmentally disabled children. By the grace of God, Scott's first classroom teacher turned out to be one of his best and we were willing to surrender our son to the special education system—at least temporarily.

The special education system, we soon learned, was in its own little universe, separate and apart from the rest of the world. It has a legal, federally mandated, mission that is superimposed over the traditional school district delivery system. Given the dreadful history that local school districts had in welcoming and educating developmentally disabled children, it's understandable they would be subordinate to state and federal laws and regulations. Left to their own devices, a great many school districts would soon disengage from this special- education mission and divert funding to other priorities. Starved for funding, the special education programs would retreat to their accustomed place at the back of the line. As it was, special advocacy groups were always in a state of high awareness to ensure that no chicanery could threaten the hard won educational advancements.

Unfortunately, this protective tent created its own set of issues. The need to establish uniform rules and regulations tends to calcify a system over time, robbing it of its freshness, vitality and flexibility. A great moral imperative degenerated into a cumbersome bureaucracy, bludgeoning the risk takers and nonconformists. A self-serving hierarchy emerged to deliver the mandated services and it became easy to lose sight of the intended beneficiary, the special education student.

It felt as though there was an uneasy alliance between special education and the balance of the School District. It stuck us that special education was the unwanted stepchild, forced on the District by a bullying federal bureaucracy. Special education siphoned money from other educational initiatives at a time when our economic survival depended on a strong, innovative and effective public school system. At least that's what a great many people were led to believe. In reality, a very significant infusion of federal funding accompanied each special education student enrolled in the public school system.

Still, local school districts contributed a certain level of funding to meet this federal mandate. It's all well and good that we welcomed developmentally disabled children into the public school system, but let's not get carried away with sentimentalism. If these outliers were robbing our normal and gifted children of critically needed educational funding, then it was time to pull up the welcome mat.

In the final analysis, school districts were not judged and evaluated based on how well they were meeting their special education goals. It wasn't really important to them if Scott has made progress in toileting or dressing or identifying picture cards. This seemed to be a peripheral responsibility, unrelated to their primary educational mission. To be sure, they wanted to adhere to the letter of the law, but for many traditional educators, the special-education mandate was an unwelcome drain on their time and resources.

So a parallel hierarchy was established to deal with the problem. It was charged with assuring that the district was in compliance with State and Federal laws. Their job was to design special education programs and ride herd on those pesky parents who were expecting miracles from a beleaguered school system. Parents with concerns and complaints were expected to navigate a byzantine bureaucracy, designed to assure that malcontents rarely found their way to their elected school boards.

While the vast majority of parents go through door number one and deal with a traditional school hierarchy, special education parents are shuffled off to door number two. Behind this door, you will find a director of special education, assistant director, special education teachers, classroom aids and a cadre of occupational, physical, speech and behavior specialists.

This team designed and implemented an individual educational program (IEP) for each special- education student. At the beginning of the year, a special- education team, comprised of the classroom teacher, classroom aides, specialists and the principal met with us to design Scott's IEP. We agreed on a set of objectives, such as "Scott will learn to put his shirt on independently, identify x number of picture cards, keep his hands off other children or go to the bathroom independently x percentage of the time". We left reasonably content, assured that the educators and specialists would develop techniques and strategies to accomplish the IEP goals and objectives.

Jean settled into a new routine that involved waking Scott up early, getting him fed, cleaned and dressed, and walking him out to greet the district's little yellow shuttle. Since Scott couldn't communicate in any meaningful way, a little notepad was used by the classroom teacher to discuss progress and concerns. This little notebook is her only way to know what's going on in the classroom, along with infrequent discussions with the classroom teacher. Too often, the information communicated back to Jean was negative. Scott had a meltdown, or Scott bit his aide, or Scott grabbed other students. It was really disconcerting because we really couldn't do anything about the problem. We had no real idea of the context in which these incidents occurred. We really hoped that significant headway was being made, but we had no way of really knowing. It was a far cry from our years and years of daily hands-on, involvement and we reluctantly stayed clear and let them do what they needed to do to accomplish the IEP goals. We can only assume that the advanced technology available to educators today allows them to keep up a much more informative dialogue with parents. If not, they should be barbequed for their insensitivity.

The IEP was one strange process. What could sound better than having a group of well- trained professionals design an individual program for our son? We were allowed to collaborate with the experts, sign off on the goals and objectives and sit back and wait for progress to materialize before our very eyes. It was comforting, a welcome respite from the years of hands- on therapy. We were in the embracing arms of a benevolent system.

Unfortunately, theory and application were once again in mortal conflict. If we saw no progress from year to year, either the theoretical construct was faulty or the application was incompetent. Either we were being spoon fed a heavy dose of nonsense or the team of teachers and specialists was simply failing to do their job. Each year, we met with a large special education team who laid out all the educational and therapeutic goals for the upcoming year. A consensus was reached between the team and ourselves and we had our kumbaya moment.

Another year passed and we were distressed that the district met few, if any, IEP objectives. It was certainly obvious to us that the Scott wasn't demonstrating any progress toward reaching the stated goals, but we were routinely assured that he was doing just fine. That is, until we met with the team at the end of the year to assess progress. We were then informed that few, if any, goals and objectives were met during the year. We were astounded that no effort was made to modify the program, discard what wasn't working and try something new. They were rigid and inflexible and completely unaccountable. If there was a complete lack of progress, well, obviously the problem was Scott. They collectively pointed their fingers at the real culprit, the one person who couldn't speak for himself. It was a disheartening display of passing the buck and deflecting responsibility and accountability.

The annual IEP meetings were a charade. We were typically outnumbered by five or ten to one, depending on just how much of a nuisance we'd made of ourselves over the preceding year. If they perceive that we were likely to hold our nose and stamp our feet, they sent in a larger group that typically included the principal, classroom teacher, specialists and even the director of special education. They seemed to listen attentively, respect our point of view and incorporate as much of our input as possible into the next IEP. It was all very civilized and accommodating, unless we dared complain about a fundamental lack of progress. At that point, they circled the wagons and assured us that they had held up their end of the bargain. They had adhered religiously to the IEP, but Scott was just not able to make any headway.

All the usual tricks are deployed by the team, from killing you with kindness and empathy to paraphrasing our concerns. Brows were furrowed, heads nodded and sympathy was expressed. We're told what great parents we were and how lucky Scott was to have such a loving home. They were convinced that significant breakthroughs were just over the horizon. We needed to trust them, be patient and have faith that progress would be made. They spent far more time placating us than admitting any failure on their part to implement an IEP that they themselves agreed was achievable.

It's was a mind numbing experience. Rather than engaging primarily in a discussion with the classroom teacher and her aides, the bulk of the IEP time was taken up by various specialists who did little more than offer counsel and advice to the classroom teacher. They seemed to have inordinate influence in developing the annual IEP. Their hands- on time with Scott was very limited because their expertise was better deployed by observing and teaching the teachers. If things got a bit heated or testy, the principal or special education administrators would step up to the plate and offer their various platitudes or rationalizations. We felt very controlled, manipulated and trivialized.

The significant majority of the annual IEP meetings were dominated by professionals other than those working directly with Scott on a daily basis. It was anathema to our belief that those closest to Scott were the real experts. This didn't mean that additional expertise shouldn't be brought to the table, but, it could be done so on a complimentary basis. The system was turned on its head, with those farthest removed and least accountable having the most influence in developing the IEP.

We knew that Scott was capable of learning and overcoming some of these developmental roadblocks. After intensive effort, he learned to walk. We taught him how to ride a three- wheeled tricycle and we were astonished to see him steer and pedal the trike around the posts in our three- car garage. That step took a degree of coordination and cognitive capability that we didn't know existed.

We also brought in to the house an independent developmental disability specialist who taught Scott how to use his hand to signal yes by moving it up and down. Twenty years later, he was still using this gross motor movement to indicate yes to a question. The district was not particularly interested in deploying this type of gross motor signing and stuck to their failed efforts to help Scott develop fine motor skills. It was a critical opportunity lost simply because they were too stubborn, proud, or incompetent to follow up.

They pursued their own program of augmented communication that involved using pictures and symbols to communicate needs and desires. There is nothing wrong with this approach, and it works with a great many developmentally disabled children. But given Scott's enormous fine- motor and cognitive limitations, it would have been a cogent move to teach him to communicate through gross motor signing. We understood the rationale behind their approach; they wanted him to communicate in a way that any normal person would understand. But this inflexibility robbed him of an opportunity to more easily communicate his most basic needs.

A truly stunning example of Scott's ability to learn during his early school years occurred on the ski slopes of Snoqualmie Pass. We had heard of a special program called Ski for All that welcomed kids of all ability levels to the ski slopes. Scott could just barely walk at that time, but we decided to take a fling and see what would happen. I sincerely wish I could remember his instructor's name because he was truly extraordinary, living proof that a good teacher with a great attitude could accomplish wonders.

The first week, Scott put on the heavy ski boots and trudged over to this young, eager volunteer instructor. We just shook our heads, convinced we were about to witness yet one more failure to accomplish anything substantive. We were on a fool's errand, reaching once again for the impossible. After taking the one hundred twenty mile round trip to the pass for the next four weeks, we were treated to our very own genuine milestone. Scott was able to traverse the baby slope on two skis without poles. He made it all the way down without falling and he appeared to be in total control of his movements. It was an exhilarating moment in our lives, a tear- jerking event. This instructor appeared to accomplish the impossible and we were awestruck. For a brief, fleeting moment, our son looked like any normal boy on the ski slope.

This kid could learn! He did so in his own way and on his own time-frame. Our collective job was to locate the safe's combination and release the contents. We needed to stretch our imaginations and open our minds to fresh approaches. He responded to the right people with the right attitude. We absolutely had to keep pushing, believing and working like maniacs. We still had time to make significant progress before the door would slam shut on his chance to lead a more independent life.

Our whole life with Scott has been spent racing the clock, frantically pursuing every opportunity to climb the next step of the developmental ladder. Paradoxically, while progress is painfully slow and intermittent, the sense of urgency magnifies. Time becomes our nemesis, unrelenting, unforgiving and inexorable.

So, quite naturally, the IEP assumed huge importance as we moved ahead with the public school experience. This was the implementation mechanism for special education and it needed to be executed with competence and enthusiasm. Special education, in itself, is a complex, maddening and frustrating phenomena. It has a moral, noble premise that is a prayer answered for generations of developmentally disabled children. These kids can now come out into the light of day and be treated as normal school-age children. They have a chance at life, an opportunity to develop to their God-given potential. We didn't take this promise and opportunity lightly.

Regrettably, legal mandates can be a two-edged sword. School districts can either comply with the letter of the law or risk financial penalties or lawsuits from angry parents. As special- education advocates push against a very strong historical bias to exclude DD children, school districts face an avalanche of reporting requirements. The law asks districts to prove that they are taking this mandate seriously, because their track record of dealing with our children is deplorable.

A lack of trust creates a burden of proof on the part of school districts nationwide. The stronger the initial resistance to change on the part of school districts, the more obstinate the regulatory agencies and advocacy groups become. School districts had better darn well leave behind a coherent paper or electronic trail. Since the agencies can't trust the districts to do the right thing, they design exacting reporting systems that assure compliance.

Unfortunately, this kind of relationship has a downside. The letter of the law and the spirit of the law become untangled. Cumbersome, inflexible bureaucracies emerge to implement the mandate. An interesting parallel comes to mind from my years of justifying park budgets to skeptical elected officials. If citizens and elected officials trust you, they demand very little proof. Conversely, if there is a lack of trust, no amount of proof is sufficient.

Scarce organizational resources can be spent on developing trust between all parties or wasted on performance audits and other schemes intended to justify organizational expenditures. Again, the more you lean toward the letter of the law, the more you straightjacket the principal players. You rob them of their initiative, flexibility and enthusiasm. The underlying moral imperative becomes submerged in a sea of red tape, and the victims, as usual, are the special- education students.

This is a convoluted way of saying that the IEP process can fall victim to form over substance. The rigid process complies with the intent of the law, but lacks both spirit and accountability. The IEP process, to us, seems comparable to a greyhound chasing a mechanical rabbit. The goals are always just out of reach, seemingly unattainable. They are dangled out there, tantalizing, tasty and elusive. Each year, we rallied for another race, received support and encouragement, and watched helplessly as our little battler fell farther and farther behind the rabbit.

A pattern has emerged over the course of Scott's young life. From hospital therapists to the birth- to- three center to the home therapy program to the early school years, overly confident experts prescribe therapeutic bromides, ask for our support and patience and achieve minimal results. The chasm between their cheery forecasts and the dreary results continued to widen. We couldn't really discern whether they meant what they said or whether they had the expertise to achieve substantive change. We were in this perpetual fog, grasping for answers. Was there any truth to be uncovered or were we in some kind of netherworld, chasing the unattainable?

Blind Alleys

We found ourselves in a totally unexpected place. We never dreamed as we undertook this grave assignment that Scott would plateau to such a degree. After finally accepting the fact that he would not lead a normal life, we assumed that he could eventually become more independent. Certainly, some day he could live independently, hold a job, have a "circle of friends", and be capable of meeting his most basic needs (toileting, eating, dressing, bathing, communicating, and interacting with others.)

We were still clinging to that Ski for All moment, hoping we could exploit some hidden strength that would create a unique identity for our son. We've all seen the Hollywood movies featuring a physically or developmentally disabled person who overcomes enormous obstacles or displays astonishing attributes. Whether we were watching Rain Main, Forest Gump or A Beautiful Mind, we were inspired by their unique personality and unexplainable talent.

However, nothing seemed to be working. We kept working that tumbler over and over on the combination, but to no avail. Desperate times required desperate measures and we started opening the door to a variety of alternative approaches. Much like the terminal cancer patient with nothing to lose, we were receptive to ideas outside the mainstream. Some were reasonable and plausible, while others were almost laughable.

We enrolled Scott in a horseback riding program for developmentally disabled children. The program claimed that the relationship between disabled children and their specially trained horses was magical. The children developed better balance and a sense of control not found in other parts of their life. They could do exactly the same thing on the horse that normal kids could do. Their self-confidence was enhanced; they develop a strong bond with the horse; they had a terrific recreation experience, and their balance and coordination improved. The program received glowing newspaper reviews and we knew of parents that raved about the experience.

Unfortunately, Scott wasn't remotely interested in getting on this big, intimidating beast. Also, as with other therapeutic interventions, the crucial variable was the relationship between the instructor and the child. A tuned- in, enthusiastic and competent teacher, aide or instructor can make all the difference in the world. Therapeutic horseback riding appeared to us to be a nice recreational outlet for developmentally disabled children, but its therapeutic value was negligible for Scott.

Jean finally said "no mas" the day one of their sainted instructors laughed at Scott when he got on the horse going the wrong way. This senior instructor yelled and laughed at one of the most developmentally disabled people she would ever meet. She should have been summarily dismissed and made to live just one day in his shoes.

Through trial and error, we have learned to be very selective as to who can work with Scott in any capacity. A nonverbal child is just too vulnerable to leave in the care of incompetent and insensitive people. Just because they are working in the field in some capacity, that is not sufficient reason to trust their empathy, judgment and capability. There is a tendency on the part of DD parents to be grateful that someone, anyone, is willing to work with and spend time with their child. We too easily overlook their shortcomings because any kind of help is greatly appreciated.

We can't wrap our heads around the fact that a certain percentage of these people are either just indifferent to the needs of our son or come with some very serious baggage. We need some kind of mechanism to screen out the incompetent or dangerous characters that seem to inhabit the dark corners of the developmental disability world. This kind of person comes from an entirely different planet. Because caregiving is so much more than a job to us, we can lose perspective and objectivity.

Interestingly, Scott will often let us know whether he wants to be around certain people by the way he responds to their presence. His reactions to people are incredibly varied, from hugs and embraces to indifference to full-fledged flight and panic. We have learned to pay close attention to these responses because he has been a fairly accurate barometer over the years. Also, he shouldn't have to be placed in the care of people he dislikes or doesn't feel comfortable around.

Experience confirmed that those organizations that did the best job of screening and training their employees and volunteers achieved the best results. With Scott, it has always boiled down to the one-on-one, hands-on, relationship. The stronger the relationship, the greater the chance of success. We learned to ignore the wild claims and hoopla of the organizations and focus instead on who was working with Scott. Were they tuned in to his personality? Did they genuinely care about him and were they working diligently to achieve results? These were always the people we respected, admired and appreciated. They were typically located near the bottom of the hierarchy, but this usually meant they knew more about our son and were in the best position to actually accomplish something.

So during these early school years, we continue to chase promising claims down blind alleys. We had that "don't leave any stone unturned" mentality, a stubborn belief that undiscovered answers were out there for those true believers willing to dig hard and deep enough.

A number of years ago, a fad known as "facilitated communication" swept the developmentally disabled community. Before delving into this program that defied credulity, let's remember that Scott has never spoken, written or read a single word. He has not demonstrated the capacity to sign or convey complex thoughts.

Facilitated communication involved placing a developmentally disabled person with no language or communication capability in front of a computer and accompanying keyboard. This person would then guide the hand of a trained facilitator magically to the appropriate letters on the keyboard to complete sentences and thoughts. At long last, the door was opened from their communication prison and they could finally tell the world what they were feeling and thinking. Across the country, miraculous results were reported of developmentally disabled people coming out of their muted shells with the help of trained facilitators. This intervention was being touted as the answer for autistic children, particularly.

To say we were skeptical would be an understatement of massive proportion. But with nothing to lose but time and credibility, we agreed to acquire one of the facilitation devices and arrange to have Scott sit with a facilitator and give it the old college try. Believe it or not, it didn't work. Someone who couldn't speak, spell, write or read somehow couldn't convey coherent sentences through the magical box. Accusations surfaced that the facilitators were guiding the fingers of the DD people and producing the publicized results. Just another example of something too good to be true for our vulnerable son.

We are not denigrating any program that might achieve results for some segment of the developmentally disabled population. Lord knows, we've tried just about anything, hoping to hit the jackpot with our version of the lottery. As they say, you can't win if you don't play, but, my goodness, we were bucking extraordinary odds.

We kept sampling other snake- oil remedies over the years. At the urging of our home therapy guru, we spent several weekends with a program called auditory training. Theoretically, we could improve Scott's capacity to hear words, sounds and phrases that might assist his ability to speak and communicate. One again, another dead end without any real merit graced our landscape. During this timeframe, there were many other examples of programs too silly to mention, but we pursued them, nevertheless, with varying degrees of enthusiasm.

Mesh to the Rescue

S cott continued to languish in a series of special- education classrooms
for several years. We were settling into a discouraging pattern of sending our son off to his special school, with a goal of reaching the various
IEP objectives. Jean would receive daily notes that would discuss what
they were working on and any behavior issues that popped up, like biting,
pulling hair, grabbing or complaining. The school didn't appear to have
any cogent answers or suggestions for dealing with his behavioral issues,
so it struck us as very odd. First, they were the trained, certified special-
education professionals. Second, what were supposed to do about whatever
behavior issues Scott was displaying at school?

It was as though all they did was observe the problem and then reported to us that it was occurring. They lacked any real imagination or
commitment to solve the problem. They were very poor at offering alternative solutions and making midcourse adjustments. It felt as though
any problems relating to behavior or failure to meet IEP goals were our
problem, and our problem exclusively. Accountability and responsibility
were not shared; the failure to progress rested exclusively with Scott and
his disillusioned parents.

We were mired in bureaucratic muck. The traditional special- education
system was strangling any hope that we retained for our son. The system
wasn't designed to achieve results. It became something of an illusion, ap-
pearing to educate, while fixating on meeting legal requirements. Yes, they

would accept our kids in special- education classrooms and, yes, they would develop IEPs. No, they wouldn't make regular adjustments to the IEP, and, no, they would not take responsibility for meeting IEP goals. The resources would be allocated, the paper trail would be established and the kids would be pushed along the conveyer belt. The kids would go from one grade to the next, whether or not they achieved a single IEP goal. Were they going to school or attending an elaborate day care? Were we dealing with professional educators or well- paid caregivers? Was this whole public school experience legitimate or were we just engaging in some fantasy?

Around this time, we heard about a pilot inclusion program (MESH) that was going to be offered at Emily Dickenson Elementary School. Developmentally disabled students would be fully integrated into regular classrooms, with the help of a full time aide. This pioneering approach was right up our alley and we immediately asked to be included. Unfortunately, the program was limited to students living within the catchment area of Emily Dickenson and we lived on the opposite side of the district. You can probably guess what we did to deal with this problem. We moved.

Along with a number of other parents that we knew from Gordon Hauck, we attended a briefing from the MESH program administrator. Her presentation was inspiring and right on point. She concluded her pitch by stating that this "was the right thing to do." Our kids had every right to be included in regular classrooms and everyone would be richer for the experience. Regular classroom students would provide excellent role models and help our kids achieve their IEP goals. Our kids, in turn, would provide a real- world example of diversity and greatly enhance everyone's perspective and tolerance. Additionally, regular classroom students and teachers would develop a deep appreciation and respect for our special kids. They would become more caring and empathetic, a gift that would last a lifetime.

She promised that teachers and students would be prepared in advance to accept our special students and she delivered on this promise. What a great contrast to years of bombastic promises that were never met! The regular classroom kids were welcoming and supportive and the classroom teacher and special aide were competent and enthusiastic. Scott spent time with the regular students on the playground, in the cafeteria and at school assemblies. He was embraced and accepted as a unique and valued human being. It was a Camelot moment, a seductive, but unsustainable, glimpse of the ideal.

It was during this first year at Emily Dickenson that we experienced something very special. One of Scott's classmates who lived in our neighborhood came by our house, knocked on the door and asked if Scott could come out and play. They went out to the backyard and played on the play equipment and just hung around together for an hour or so. This boy was very kind, patient and understanding. This was the first and last time anyone every came over to our house to play with Scott. Friendships are ultimately grounded in mutual interests, common experiences and some level of intellectual parity. It's heartbreaking to know that our son will never have close friends, play on a soccer or baseball team, go to a sleepover, attend a summer camp, or star in the school play. But on this special day, time stood still and a friend came over to play.

We have come to learn that respect and appreciation of diversity is not just some hollow liberal refrain. It's not simply political correctness. For those of us on the outside looking in, it's an affirmation that our loved one is valued and accepted. As Scott has grown and his differences become more obvious and pronounced, he stands out in a crowd. He walks on his toes, needs an arm to hang on to for balance and puts his hands in his mouth. Wherever we go, whether to the grocery store, restaurant or swimming pool, he attracts his share of gawking and attention. Since we are the type of people who prefer to be anonymous in a crowd, this used to make us acutely uncomfortable. Over the years, we've grown immune to this overt attention and we understand that it is simply the type of curiosity that captivates people as they pass a traffic accident on the freeway. It's nothing personal, just a casual interest in someone who looks and acts differently from the rest of us. To view this curiosity any differently would be to fall into a paranoia trap. We have absolutely no way of knowing what people are really thinking and, really, does it make any difference?

The more young people, in particular, are exposed to the developmentally disabled, the more this type of scrutiny will diminish. It won't be that big of a deal to them because they were exposed to our kids at a young age and have come to accept them as an integral part of the human family. It's the type of respect and acceptance that minorities have been struggling to achieve for a very long time in this country. It's a battle that will always be fought and will probably never be won to our complete satisfaction. While it's asking a lot of human nature, progress will be made incrementally and life will get better for our loved ones.

This climate of acceptance spilled over to our new neighborhood. Neighbors were incredibly welcoming to Scott and our entire family. We became part of an enlightened community that included both the school and neighborhood. For the first time in ten years, we began to relax and ease off on the advocacy accelerator. It was probably nothing more than a self-induced illusion, but we felt like a normal family. Scott thrived in this environment and we spent the next several years in a very contented place.

Scott proceeded seamlessly from the third to the fifth grade and we were impressed with the diligence exercised in achieving IEP goals and integrating Scott into the school family. He received achievement certificates, communication from school personnel was positive and supportive and he continued to make progress. We were realistic enough to understand that he would never bridge the gap between himself and his age- appropriate peers, but we were optimistic that he could ultimately achieve a higher level of independence and function. We believed that we were collectively involved in a noble and attainable cause.

These were the halcyon years, never to be duplicated. We will always remember them fondly and we have great admiration for the teachers, aides and MESH administrators. It was a heroic effort on behalf of society's most challenged and vulnerable. For a fleeting moment, hope was restored, and a special life was honored. Here's to the good guys, wherever they may be twenty- five years later!

When Scott entered the sixth grade, his final year at Emily Dickenson, the rails came off the track. The odds finally caught up with us and we drew the retro teacher with a bad attitude. Communication to and from the school started to take on a negative tone and we began to feel distinctly uncomfortable. We were particularly concerned about making headway on his IEP goals relating to toileting. We had been working relentlessly on getting him toilet trained for seven years and still had not achieved total success. He was improving and success appeared to be a possibility.

So off we went on a final, last minute drive to get Scott toilet trained. We were told repeatedly by special-education people that continence would be enormously beneficial to Scott in terms of social acceptance and eligibility for independent living and employment. We were still harboring hopes that Scott could be elevated to a higher, more self-sufficient plane. To have any chance of reaching this next level of independence, he absolutely had to conquer this incontinence barrier. If we collectively failed to achieve this modest goal, what hope did he have for a more independent life?

The school district brought in a behavior psychologist to evaluate Scott and make specific toileting recommendations. We also sent Scott to a Group Health interdisciplinary team for an extensive medical assessment. Both parties concluded that Scott could achieve toileting success and recommended that we take him out of diapers and training pants and put him in regular underwear. This would signal to Scott that we had higher expectations for success. He would also be able to feel his accidents and be more likely to initiate trips to the toilet.

He made significant progress through the first three-quarters of his final year at Emily Dickenson. He had fewer and fewer accidents at school and home after we put him in regular underwear. We were finally on the cusp of defeating this longtime nemesis. We were in something of a panic to achieve this goal before we placed him in the "Junior High School Zoo"—for obvious reasons.

But then, at the last possible moment, Emily Dickenson failed Scott and his family. Jean discovered one spring afternoon that Scott had come home in a diaper and wondered what in the world was happening. It turns out that some third- rate, utterly incompetent, occupational therapist decided that school staff would not change Scott unless he was wearing in diaper or training pants. Claiming a public health risk, she recruited the school principal to her side and we were broadsided with this monumentally irresponsible decision at a special meeting in the principal's office.

We were stunned and flabbergasted. How could they change direction on a dime and ignore the recommendations of their own psychologist and the Group Health interdisciplinary team? How could they summarily dismiss the major breakthrough in his toileting? After Jean spent day after day after day administering suppositories at six in the morning, they just disregarded all the backbreaking work because of a trumped-up hygiene issue? What in the world were they thinking? His future was of so little importance that they couldn't be momentarily inconvenienced? For the occasional accident, they had the requisite rubber gloves and change of clothing, so sanitation and hygiene would not be compromised.

We argued and argued, but our pleas fell on deaf, ignorant ears. They were smug and condescending. This was a failure in moral leadership, a repudiation of the MESH philosophy. Almost immediately, after Scott was placed in diapers, his toileting success plummeted. He was virtually given permission to remain incontinent. His school toileting regime was now out of sync with our home program and our chance to achieve a major developmental breakthrough was irretrievably lost. He regressed rapidly, and despite persistent efforts to address the problem, we couldn't get over the hump. We kept at it for another sixteen years, but we finally admitted defeat when he reached thirty years of age.

It's hard to put in words how disappointed and disillusioned we were with the school Principal and special education administrators who supported the position of the occupational therapist and classroom teacher. They deprived our son of his one chance at continence and left us with a caregiving burden for the rest of our life. It was unforgivable, petty and unprofessional. They took the easy way out at the worst possible time, and Scott and his family paid the price.

What a sad, inexplicable ending to an otherwise magnificent experience at Emily Dickenson. From that point forward, we were pushing a boulder uphill with the school district and we never again had the same belief in the public school system. We were slapped in the face with the ugly truth that Scott's long- term well-being was of secondary importance to this educational establishment. We would have to strap on our protective armor and resume our battle with an intransigent special- education hierarchy. What a completely unnecessary waste of time and energy!

The Ripple Effect

The purpose of life is not to be happy. It is to be useful, to be honorable, to be compassionate, and to have it make some difference that you have lived and lived well

— Ralph Waldo Emerson

Living with Scott at times resembles watching a rock thrown into a calm body of water. The concentric waves reach farther and farther out from the initial point of impact, leaving a large area influenced by a small disturbance. Scott has had a major residual influence on a great many people, from fellow students and neighborhood kids to teachers, aides, caregivers and family. Once you make the decision to enter his life, your life is changed immediately. It's like Einstein said about entanglement, a quirky phenomenon in quantum physics, "it's spooky at a distance."

Whether you cite quantum physics, Buddhist philosophy or Judeo-Christian theology, we are all integrally connected and our interactions have far reaching influence and consequences. For example, Scott inspired us to champion various causes that benefited the developmentally disabled. Jean assumed responsibility as co-chair of the state chapter of the national home therapy organization. We were active in the Support a Child auction which distributed funds to a variety of agencies serving the developmentally disabled. We were involved in assorted parent coalitions that provided information and assistance to families of developmentally disabled children. Without Scott's inspiration, we would never have made these contributions.

My entire career trajectory was influenced by Scott. Because of Scott's acute needs, occupational stability was of paramount importance. I abandoned my professional aspiration to become a city manager and, instead, devoted my talent and energy to parks and recreation. It turned out to be a far better fit for my personality and skill set and, at the risk of sounding terminally self-serving, I do believe that Bellevue developed one of the premier suburban park systems in the United States. Without question, Scott had a direct impact on the evolution of the Bellevue Park system.

Perhaps Scott's greatest residual contribution to the world was the creation of an expanded special-recreation program within the City of Bellevue's Park and Recreation Department. As director of this city agency, I was never particularly interested in or concerned with this quaint little program. It was pretty much out of sight and out of mind, although it was quietly championed by Cheryl Mellor, a recreation specialist with a social conscience and genuine affinity for the developmentally disabled. The program was operating almost clandestinely out of second- rate facilities, from church basements to run- down recreation buildings. It was the neglected stepchild, getting by on whatever chump change we were willing to divert from higher- priority programs.

Cheryl was valiantly organizing Special Olympics activities, social activities and various recreation classes for this neglected population, but her achievements were basically ignored and unappreciated by the department. The department was clearly lagging behind the curve on recognizing and valuing the developmentally disabled in our community and I plead guilty to turning a blind eye to this population.

When Scott arrived on the scene, my level of awareness, concern and interest skyrocketed. I was appalled by the blatant discrimination experienced by our most vulnerable and underserved. I became a convert to the cause and became determined to make up for lost time. We immediately allocated additional funding to expand program offerings, and we began to look seriously at finding a first-rate building that developmentally disabled people could use on a priority basis.

The long- range park and recreation plan was amended to include program and facility improvements for special recreation. The City's capital-improvement program and park- bond issues included funding for major building renovations to accommodate this program.

A breakthrough finally occurred when the city was presented with the opportunity to purchase a sizeable building being vacated by the Elks Club. This one- level, modern building was ideally suited for our senior program which was occupying an older community center. Staff recommended the relocation of the senior program to this new building and simultaneously recommended that the existing building, the Highland Center, be renovated and used on a priority basis by the city's special -recreation program. This recommendation was approved by the Bellevue City Council, and the city finally elevated special recreation to the status it so richly deserved. It was a paradigm shift, one that ushered in a new era of respect for a special and long- neglected constituency.

Before too long, the city allocated over two million dollars to provide building additions and renovations and full and part- time staffing levels increased dramatically. Several hundred DD children and adults were offered a wide range of recreation programs, including day camps, Special Olympics, arts, crafts, theater, trips and tours and social evenings out on the town.

Two Highland Center moments are burned into my memory. The first moment was the inaugural production of *West Side Story* starring a cast of Highland Center participants. This stirring and moving musical was directed by a woman with an incredible capacity to get the very most out of every cast member, from those with very minor cognitive limitations to the more profoundly affected. The play took place in the prestigious Convention Center Theater in front of a packed house of friends and family. The actors performed just magnificently up to their various ability levels and there were plenty of tears in the house as the final curtain came down. They proved something very important that night to themselves and everyone in attendance. Their talent was genuine, their enthusiasm unmatched and their confidence elevated. It was a night I will never forget.

I also remember as if it were yesterday watching a group of about twenty adult DD people waiting to get on a special van to participate in their Friday Night Out. This was an organized special program in which reasonably high functioning adult DD persons went out to dinner and a show on Friday night. They looked forward to this social outing all week long and very obviously enjoyed getting together with their peers. Without the organizing prompt from the Highland Center, these folks would have been spending Friday night at home with their parents or group- home caregivers. The Highland Center went a very long way toward reducing social isolation and loneliness among DD adults in the Bellevue community.

The program was a real shot in the arm to the Bellevue DD community and it was quickly emulated by a number of other cities in Washington State. The program established such a national reputation that it received the National Recreation and Park Association Gold Medal Award for special recreation.

Scott is obviously the inspiration for this book. To whatever extent this book influences positive changes in the lives of the developmentally disabled and their families, Scott is the wellspring.

A very significant number of lives were enhanced as a direct result of the influence that one nonverbal child had on his parents and others who interacted with him during his life. What a great testimonial to the value of each human life. We were Scott's instrument of change, and believe me, it would have never happened without his indomitable spirit. Our eyes were propped open and directed toward an acute need. At the risk of sounding melodramatic, we think that God works through his most vulnerable children to make the rest of us better people. The world is a better place because they are among us.

A Life Worth Living

*Always remember that you are absolutely unique, just like
everyone else.*

— MARGARET MEAD

This discussion leads to an even more fundamental observation. A guillotine hovers over embryos that are confirmed by genetic testing to be "damaged and abnormal" before they emerge from the womb. A lifetime of sacrifice, despair and heartache will inevitably follow the family unless they make a sensible decision to abort the fetus. Right? Let's just get rid of the defective child and hope for better luck next time. We can all breathe easier knowing that we won't have to endure years and years of parenting a special- needs child who may never reach normal milestones, meet our lofty expectations, or bear a physical resemblance to the family tree.

Had we been in a position to make this life and death decision about Scott, we probably would have taken the easy route and elected to terminate the pregnancy. This decision would certainly have altered our lives dramatically, allowing us to stay in the predictable, conventional lane. Our lives would lack the depth and texture that Scott made possible. His gift to us has been immeasurable, highlighted by our enhanced capacity to love, empathize and contribute. Like so many developmentally disabled persons, he lights up our life. He adds meaning and purpose and has his own special place in the universe.

Let's just take Down syndrome as an example. An NBC article authored by Kimberly Hayes Taylor illustrates just how archaic attitudes can be downright dangerous. She describes the results of three studies conducted by the Boston Children's Hospital.

" In the first study, out of 2044 parents or guardians surveyed, seventy nine percent reported their outlook on life was more positive because of their child with Down syndrome.

"A second study found 97 percent of siblings expressed feelings of pride for their brother or sister and 88 percent were convinced that they were better people because of their sibling.

"A third study focused on feelings and attitudes of people with Down syndrome. 99 percent said they were happy with their lives, 97 percent said they liked who they were and 96 percent said they liked the way they look."

Yet, a surprisingly high percentage of prospective Down syndrome parents make the decision to terminate the pregnancy. This is an intensely personal decision with many interlocking variables. We only hope that careful consideration is given to the fact that the developmentally disabled and their immediate families can lead happy and productive lives. It should not be a knee jerk, no brainer, decision based on prejudice and fear.

I would like to cite a couple of other examples of how intolerant modern society can be toward the physically and developmentally disabled. According to a November 5, 2014 Galaxy report, a recent UK court case has allowed a mother to end the life of her 12 year- old- daughter. "The decision constitutes an extremely troubling legal precedent, the report says," representing for the first time the British legal system has allowed a child breathing on her own, not on life support and not diagnosed with a terminal illness, to be killed by the medical system."

"Nancy Fitzmaurice was a blind girl born with hydrocephalus, meningitis and septicaemia, which prevented her from walking, talking, eating or drinking independently. Her mother argued that the decision was made to end her daughters suffering, her feeding tube was withdrawn and she died of dehydration."

"Euthanasia of people with disabilities is an extremely dangerous precedent and wholly inappropriate solution to inadequate pain management, according to the autistic self- advocacy network."

A Washington State jury recently awarded 50 million dollars to the parents of a developmentally disabled boy with a genetic abnormality. Apparently, the parents, both educators, were aware that a cousin of the father had a genetic defect that resulted in a developmental disability. After becoming pregnant, they immediately sought counseling from a regional hospital and underwent genetic testing through a private testing service. If the results came back positive for this genetic condition, their stated intent was to immediately abort the fetus.

The test results were negative, they proceeded with the pregnancy and guess what? Apparently, the testing process was flawed and the baby was born with the unwanted genetic deficiency. He is now four and a half years old, unable to run or climb stairs and has a vocabulary of less than 30 words. He will require 24/7 care and support for the rest of his life and will never lead a "normal" life. This sound like anyone you've been reading about in this memoir?

How interesting and instructive! Here, a couple are awarded 50 million dollars to care for a child with a higher level of functioning than Scott. This questionable award basically says, loud and clear, that this life has negative value, a $50 million dollar burden to the family. Explicitly, the plaintiff and the jury are stating that a terrible wrong was inflicted upon the parents by the hospital and testing service. This loving family was denied the opportunity to abort a life that apparently holds no value for either the family or society.

Granted, this life will need intensive support, but he is still perfectly capable of receiving and returning love and positively influencing the lives of those within his orbit. 50 million dollars to help care for a developmentally disabled person for life? Really? That award is far in excess of the actual caregiving cost associated with this child, so the bulk of the award has to be for "pain and suffering."

Having raised a son for 34 years with substantially greater challenges than those described for this biological son of "wronged" parents, we are deeply saddened by the implication that their child will not bring them a degree of joy, happiness, perspective or unconditional love. They could just as easily have given birth to one of the legions of "normal" people who evolve into hateful, selfish personalities, lacking in empathy, compassion, innocence, and love.

Our son, while incredibly demanding and challenging at times, is a pure soul, utterly lacking in guile and deceit. I've often told people that Scott returned my soul to me and what greater gift could one person give another? Who should be giving whom 50 million dollars? Could it be that this "flawed" child will return far more than he receives? Who gets to decide whether a life has value and a capacity to give and contribute?

Taken to its logical conclusion, as genetic testing makes more and more progress, developmentally disabled people with a genetic basis for their condition will disappear from the face of "civilized society." It's not as though we are saving them from a life of pain and suffering. Rather, we are saying that they have no intrinsic value.

This is quite different from investing in scientific research that has as its objective identifying treatments and interventions that can ameliorate or eliminate many of the challenges confronting the developmentally disabled. Science and technology need to be guided by a strong moral compass. There is no question that technological and scientific "progress" are far out in front of public policy. At times, it appears as though the political/legislative, moral/ethical and scientific/technological realms operate in totally different planes from each other. Genuinely inspired public policy should synthesize the three and produce a Solomon-like wisdom that would protect our most vulnerable people.

Otherwise, the developmentally disabled will become a historical footnote, victims of a form of genocide. An entire branch of the human family will be pruned, and we will all be poorer as a result. To quote a recent editorial from Nicholas Kristof, "in the policy realm, one of the most important decisions we humans will have to make is whether to allow gene line modification. This might eliminate certain diseases, ease suffering, and make our offspring smarter and more beautiful. But it would also change our species. It would enable the wealthy to concoct superchildren. It's exhilarating and terrifying."

All we can tell the world with certainty is that Scott has genuinely loved his life. It's been unconventional and challenging, but, without a doubt, it has been worth living. He welcomes each day with a childish enthusiasm. We could all use a refresher course on how to make the most of our lives and Scott should be our professor emeritus.

It's All About Choice

The Highland Center represented a distinct philosophy, one guided by the concept of choice. Most parents of DD children want their kids to be integrated to the maximum extent possible. They want them to have the same opportunities to participate in school, sports, church, recreation and other community endeavors as their "normal" peers. If they can thrive and prosper in normal classrooms, sports activities and social events, then, by all means, they should be given that choice.

Sometimes the push toward full inclusion can become overzealous. We are obviously in the camp that wants all of our kids to be included and integrated as seamlessly as possible into society. Figuratively, we fought and bled for that right for over thirty years. We don't want artificial limits imposed on our son's future, whether those limits involve school, housing, recreation or housing. We endorse the ideal, while simultaneously recognizing reality.

There is a very understandable tendency on the part of those pushing for major social change to obliterate the status quo and assume it has no redeeming value. Rather than standing on the shoulders of those who preceded us and improving our condition incrementally, we push for radical change. We arrogantly dismiss the accomplishments of prior generations and insist that everyone embrace a new approach that is obviously more enlightened.

Developmental disability advocates have pushed the envelope over the past fifty years from total exclusion to a form of "separate but equal" to full inclusion. It's been a long, arduous fight. On the education front, they have pushed for full classroom inclusion, much like Scott experienced at Emily Dickenson. On the housing front, they have advocated aggressively against state-supported residential institutions that warehoused and dehumanized developmentally disabled people. As this option gradually faded in favor of adult family homes and group homes, advocates began a push to place the DD in the least restrictive community housing options, like apartments, rental houses, and condominiums.

In the employment arena, DD folks moved from total unemployment to sheltered workshops to fully supported employment to independent employment. In the recreation field, the new direction is to emulate education's full- inclusion model. Separate special- recreation facilities and programs are being phased out in favor of including all developmentally disabled participants in regularly offered activities. Special assistance will be provided to DD people as they participate alongside the other participants, but they won't be segregated and forced to interact exclusively with their DD peers.

The odd exception to this rule is Special Olympics. For some reason, it's recognized in this instance that DD participants need to compete against one another in a different competitive format. You know the drill, everyone participates in whatever way they can and everyone is a winner. It has a long, successful track record, a staple of everyday life for legions of the developmentally disabled. They can experience, in their own unique way, the thrill and joy of athletic participation and competition. There is no pretense that they can compete on elite baseball, track or basketball teams. They have clear physical and mental limitations that preclude competing at this level.

This arrow of change and progress that points toward full inclusion of the developmentally disabled in normal life activities is a good and honorable thing. It's vitally important to those DD people who could be characterized as being at the higher end of the developmental spectrum. No one wants to be shackled and restrained. They want the opportunity to reach their full, undiluted potential. They don't want to be perceived as their diagnosis, but rather as normal human beings. They want to be viewed as "people first" and not as some demeaning label that forever defines and limits their future.

Unfortunately, the developmentally disabled array along a very broad spectrum and not everyone can take full advantage of the full- inclusion ideal. The pendulum has swung wildly from a past characterized by indiscriminate exclusion to a present focused on full inclusion. This is entirely understandable. Substantive change demands aggressive, unrelenting advocacy, and to the true believers, it's anathema to settle for gradual change. We should know; we were once the standard- bearers for radical change.

Regrettably, in all areas of human interaction, hierarchies tend to evolve and prosper. It's no different when it comes to the physically and developmentally disabled. We originally envisioned that the Highland Center could provide a first class space available on a priority basis to both the DD and physically disabled populations. Both groups had been relegated to second class facilities and given minimal resources to conduct their programs. The physically disabled displayed a wide array of conditions, from spinal cord injuries to Parkinson's, strokes, and cardiac trauma.

We soon learned that those participants who had once been fully functioning, independent people, but now were more dependent, were absolutely determined to avoid being associated in any way with the developmentally disabled. They were appalled by the prospect of being perceived as mentally challenged. They were just as sharp as everyone else and they didn't want anyone thinking they were somehow mentally impaired because of their physical disability. They certainly wanted accommodations made for their physical limitations, but in no way, shape, or form did they want to be lumped in with the DD population.

So the experiment of lumping the two populations in the same facility was not all that enlightening from their perspective. In my opinion, this is a normal reaction, as long as it is not accompanied by a disdain and intolerance for the developmentally disabled. Unfortunately, this wasn't always the case. I had assumed, since they were fighting their own valiant battle for inclusion and acceptance, that they would have a fairly high level of affinity for the developmentally disabled. However, a surprisingly large number of physically disabled participants were anxious to put as much distance between themselves and the developmentally disabled as possible. Perhaps unwittingly, they were engaging in precisely the same type of discriminatory behavior that they were fighting against in their own life. Discouraging, but understandable, given their unique circumstances.

This hierarchy problem was not just limited to the physically versus the developmentally disabled. It persisted within the ranks of the

developmentally disabled, as well. The higher- functioning DD population and their advocates, have always pushed aggressively for those programs and services that would meet their needs. That's to be expected.
Much of the recent, presumably enlightened, push toward full inclusion
in education, employment, recreation and housing benefits those on the
higher rungs of the developmental ladder.

Without a doubt, every developmentally disabled person should have
the opportunity to "be everything they can be." Artificial barriers should
not be tolerated and full and partial inclusion should be celebrated. But this
doesn't mean that those with more profound cognitive disabilities should
be left on the sidelines without access to services that once were available to
them. In this frantic rush to ensure that those at the top get access to full
inclusion, those at the bottom can be given short shrift.

Sure, all the right things are said about *everyone* having the ability to
participate in fully integrated programs and services, but this is just disingenuous. Not everyone can benefit from independent and supported employment, recreation, education and housing. Some need very intensive
support and intervention and, yes, special programs and facilities. Their
level of need is substantially greater than that of their higher- functioning
peers and it's just folly to assume they can be folded seamlessly into society.

This is where choice comes into play. We know for a fact that we don't
want advocates for high functioning Down syndrome or autistic children
making decisions for us on what range of services will be available to our
son. We don't want existing or potential services limited by a rigid, biased
dogma. We want choices available to us and to him: we don't want them
taken off the board because of a perceived inconsistency with full inclusion. This is fundamentally illogical and can easily result in greater isolation and exclusion for those DD people needing extensive support and the
company of peers.

Give all of our DD children and adults a fair chance at happiness and
fulfillment. If they can participate on normal athletic teams with minimal

assistance, then that's what they should do. If they would rather participate with peers through Special Olympics, that should be available to them, as well. If they can participate effectively in the school drama production, that option should be pursued. If they would be more comfortable or capable of participating in a special musical performance conducted at the Highland Center, that option should also be available. If they integrate socially with "normal" peers, that should happen wherever possible. If they would rather go out to dinner and a movie with DD peers, that should be available and encouraged. If they simply need someone to take them out to the store or a park on a one-on- one on basis, then that option should be on the table.

You get the picture. Options should be widely available for a wide spectrum of the developmentally disabled. No matter how high functioning and independent, virtually all developmentally disabled people will need a lifetime of special support and assistance. A substantial number of DD advocates do not share or accept this conclusion. They still fervently desire to reach for the stars and permanently leave the developmental disability and all that it represents in the rearview mirror. We understand. We've lived this life and still believe that we had a moral responsibility to do everything in our power to shed this albatross.

But at some point there comes a time to accept reality, embrace the differences and get on with our lives. Our son came into this world in his own little vessel, with a special journey to complete. He is not like everyone else, and he never will be. He has a different mission and our job is to open our hearts and minds to his special purpose.

We need to support one another and demonstrate empathy and concern for all developmentally disabled people. We need to work collaboratively on legislative, financial, educational, employment, recreational, and living initiatives that benefit everyone. Let's provide choices and options that make the world more acceptable and livable for our loved ones.

Those choices are what the Highland Center was all about, and it was a resounding success. Scott influenced its creation and hundreds and hundreds of participants and their families benefited. His influence continued to radiate, despite his profound limitations. Every life matters and Scott is exhibit number one.

The Crash Landing

We knew the day of reckoning was on the horizon. The MESH program was designed to serve elementary aged children in normal classrooms. Eventually, our kids would have to "graduate" from Emily Dickenson, along with all their classmates. It was time to move along to that prepubescent cauldron we euphemistically called Evergreen Junior High School. We hoped and prayed the Emily Dickenson students would continue to protect our son and educate kids entering the junior high from other elementary schools.

We also knew that theory and practice were on a collision course at the junior high school. Over the years, Scott had fallen further and further behind his peers on all academic fronts. He still had no effective avenue of communication. Emily Dickenson had robbed him of his chance at continence. His balance, stamina and behavior were less than optimum. He couldn't read, write or do any type of math whatsoever. He couldn't participate in sports, music or any other normal school activity. He was about to enter the proverbial lions' den and we were petrified. How would he be accepted and treated by kids who were entering those notorious junior high school years?

By this time the entire school district had officially adopted the inclusion model and every school was mandated to develop individual education plans that worked toward this objective. It all started feeling counterintuitive to us. How in the world would he be able to attend as many as seven different classes in seven different classrooms during the course of the day?

What would he do in an English, math, history or foreign language class? Wouldn't he just sit in the back of the classroom with his aide working on modest IEP goals? Where, precisely, did the inclusion and junior high school curriculum intersect? How could other students view him as a peer when he was so profoundly disabled?

Just at this crucial time in his life when we needed the most insightful leadership and competence, we received the polar opposite. The principal and classroom teacher were clueless, a regular keystone- cop tandem. The school still retained its special- education classroom structure and it had made no effort to adapt its curriculum to the inclusion model. The classroom teacher was new to the profession and overwhelmed with this strange new mandate. She had not done any preliminary planning or preparation to adapt her curriculum and daily schedule to this very foreign concept. It was a classic left- hand, right- hand quandary. It was as though the central administration and junior high school had never had a discussion of any kind about inclusion and how it would be adapted to a junior high environment.

We received absolutely no communication from the junior high school in advance of Scott's first day of school. Jean called the classroom teacher several times prior to the big day and received vague, ill-defined assurances that they had everything under control. *Don't worry, relax. He is in good hands. Just send him to school on the bus, and we will take it from there. We will meet in due time to formulate his individual education program, so just chill out, and we will be in touch.*

This cavalier attitude was off- putting and completely inconsistent with the MESH approach that we regarded so highly at Emily Dickenson. The faculty and student body at Emily Dickenson were prepared to receive and accept our special kids. They were educated about special needs and they welcomed our children to their school community. Parents were welcomed to interact with MESH staff, the school principal and classroom teachers.

The place felt safe and welcoming and we had no reservations about sending Scott to this school.

When you have a nonverbal child with severe cognitive limitations, you fear for his safety and well-being. There is an omnipresent fear of physical, emotional or sexual abuse by adults or other students who might view our kids as easy targets. We fear ridicule and harassment and want to be assured that our kids are going to a safe place. After all, it's extremely difficult to get a reliable reading from Scott as to whether or not he is being properly treated and respected. We have to rely on others to guarantee his safety, so we need to feel comfortable with those people who have his life in their hands a good part of the day.

This is no idle, paranoid concern. We are bombarded by newscasts or articles that describe abuse of developmentally disabled children and adults at state institutions, group homes, schools and work settings. Ironically, in February of 2015, we read about five high school football players arrested for sodomizing a special- education student. The high school where the incident occurred is within the Lake Washington School District, the same district that introduced us to the MESH program. Just one more example of why we need eternal diligence when it comes to our children. Nothing can be taken for granted: there will always be those monsters ready and willing to take advantage of our vulnerable kids and adults. When you hand your fragile child over to another person, you are still responsible for that child's welfare. It's you job to assure his or her safety and security and so you had better be assured that you are doing the right thing. It's a grave responsibility.

So, we had absolutely no idea how Scott would be integrated into this scary, overwhelming school environment. None of our initial questions and concerns were addressed in advance of the first day of school. After Jean pestered the classroom teacher with questions that she couldn't seem to answer, her calls were routed to the principal. The principal, in turn, was no better informed or helpful than the classroom teacher, but she made it clear that Jean's requests for information were unwelcome. This was a textbook example of an organization rallying around its weak link and defending itself against charges of incompetency. Under no circumstances were they primarily concerned with the welfare and education of our son. Their energy and resources were marshalled to defend the institution. Who were we to demand answers and accountability? They were the experts and we just needed to back off and give them space to do their job.

To say the least, we expected far more from this principal, who happen to be both female and a racial minority. We presumed that she had gone through her own share of discrimination and insensitivity over the course of her career and would demonstrate a modicum of fairness. It was just the opposite. She didn't want either her teachers or herself to be pressured or challenged. All the school personnel were bullheaded and uncompromising, a direct reflection of their leadership. Compromise and conciliation were obviously not core values. The idea that they were actually public servants must have seemed laughable to this retrograde regime.

This petty tyrant of a principal stooped to an all- time low to establish her dominance and control. She called Jean up and threatened her with a lawsuit alleging harassment. Can you imagine the audacity of a school principal bullying the parent of a profoundly disabled student? This specious threat was all calculated theater, designed to put us in our place. It was unconscionable and indefensible, a firing offense. We are still fuming twenty five- years later.

This lovely beginning led to a big showdown at the OK Corral. As mentioned previously, school districts are legally mandated to develop an individual education program for each special- education student. This program must be developed cooperatively and in consultation with the parents of the student. We were notified of the date and time of the IEP meeting and informed that this black- tie affair would be attended by the classroom teacher, various specialists, the principal, assistant director of special education and the director of special education for the District. We were surprised that they left out the school board and school superintendent.

While we were always badly outnumbered at our prior IEP meetings, we never felt threatened or intimidated because we were all on the same page. Also, we are not exactly the shy and retiring types, so it wasn't too difficult to hold our own if necessary. But this was different. It was a blatant attempt to intimidate and establish a pattern of dominance. At one point in the meeting the special education director for the district told Jean to be quiet and listen when she attempted to correct one of their numerous errors of fact. The entire meeting was a farce, and we left angry and embittered.

We were so damn fed up with this house of fools that we opted to hire a highly regarded disability rights attorney to accompany us to a follow- up IEP meeting. While we probably didn't achieve anything terribly noteworthy as a result of this representation, it did serve to even the intimidation scales a bit and provide notice that we would not back off when it came to our son's future. Sometimes, an overwhelming display of power needs to be met in kind and this was one of those times.

So out of this quagmire came an IEP that defined Scott's goals and objectives for the school year. He still primarily spent his time in a spe- cial- education classroom and communication from the classroom and administration was limited and primarily negative. The notes coming back home focused almost exclusively on what Scott was doing wrong— biting, grabbing, and disrupting the classroom. They couldn't seem to grasp the idea that there was an underlying cause for the behavior and no effort was made to identify the source of the problem. The beloved principal would even corner my daughter in the hallway and tell her all about Scott's issues at school. It was clearly a hostile and unproductive environment for our son and we wanted to get clear of this mess as soon as possible. This entire school experience was light years removed from the golden era of Emily Dickenson and it was hard to understand how the same school district could house two schools within a stone's throw of one another that we were so diametrically opposite.

This whole miserable experience highlighted an important lesson that we learned over the years. Those people who care the most, exhibit a reasonable degree of creativity and take the time to know Scott are the most successful educators. It doesn't matter whether they are his personal aides, classroom teachers or a specialists of some kind. Those closest to him on a daily basis matter the most and those farthest removed matter the least. Those who are highly compensated and credentialed to the hilt are relatively meaningless. They are the official guardians of the special-education system, assuring that procedures and laws are properly followed. But they are not the heart and soul of the special- education experience for students or their parents. That responsibility lies with those who actually work in the trenches and plug away on a day- to -day basis. You know, the ones who really care.

This axiom was never more apparent than when we gathered annually with the "gang" to evaluate the progress from the previous year's IEP and develop new goals and objectives for the following year. Invariably, those who spent the least amount of time with Scott used up most of the airtime. We would hear from principals, special-education administrators and a variety of specialists (occupational, speech, physical therapy) for most of the time. The classroom teacher and Scott's personal aide would be relatively silent, accepting their place in this rather bizarre caste system.

Sometimes, the IEP experience was downright otherworldly. We very consistently asked and pleaded for the IEP to emphasize communication because we couldn't see how Scott could make any progress until he could communicate more effectively. Every school district has within its stable of specialists a speech therapist. We presumed that a variety of things had to occur physically and cognitively before Scott could begin to speak. The speech therapist seemed to be the logical person to develop a pre-speech program, but we were politely and a bit condescendingly informed that speech therapists only worked with kids who were already speaking. Carrying this approach to its logical conclusion means you could not teach the alphabet until the child was already reading or teach numbers until they could calculate. At times, we felt like the character played by Alan Bates in the *King of Hearts*, in which he escapes from a mental institution, only to be shown later banging stark naked on the door of the asylum, asking to be let back in. It didn't feel like we belonged in the real world.

Time was running out on Scott and this hostile institution headed up by Nurse Ratchet was not the place for him at this time in his life. We heard from other special-education parents in the district that another junior high school a few miles to the south was far more progressive and welcoming. With nothing to lose but three more years in the house of horrors, we petitioned the special- education administrator for a change of schools. Understanding that transportation could be a constraint, we offered to accept this responsibility. However, once again proving our theorem, the central office turned us down flat. Whether this was in retaliation for our past misdeeds or simple bureaucratic inertia, we will never know. Again, Scott's best interest was not the primary consideration. They were in charge, and it was about time we accepted that fact!

Unwilling to be shoved around by the intellectual deadbeats in special education, we wrote a long letter to the school superintendent pleading our case one more time. If this request fell on deaf ears, we were prepared to appeal to the school board and make a media stink. We were ready to become the loud and obnoxious squeaky wheel because Scott needed us to stay strong and advocate on his behalf. To our genuine surprise and delight, the school superintendent approved our request. Oddly, our encounters with that portion of the district separate and apart from the special education administrators were generally positive and supportive. We remain grateful to the school superintendent, for evaluating our request on its merits and overriding his petty and incompetent managers.

Mercifully, we were able to migrate from the ridiculous to the sublime. His new junior high school had a very positive, supportive and welcoming administration and classroom teacher. His aide was absolutely superb and we once again felt that he was in good hands when we put him on the little yellow bus each morning. It was apparent that everyone was doing their very best to implement the IEP goals and he was integrated as effectively as possible into the school environment. The teacher and special education coordinator for the junior high school communicated very well. They sent home positive summaries, answered all phone calls quickly and constructively and made us feel like we were important contributors to his IEP. What a difference!

It was abundantly clear to us that full educational inclusion was a bit of a pipedream at this level and that the best we could hope for was that he could be included whenever and wherever it made sense. Otherwise, the school would work diligently on his IEP goals, communicate with us on a consistent and positive basis and assure that he was safe and respected. The new junior high school delivered across the board.

Despite the vastly improved educational environment, Scott's educational progress was very limited and intermittent. He seemed to have reached a developmental plateau. While he did add a few things to his skill set, like riding a three-wheel bike and identifying and using some picture symbols, his educational development stagnated. He seemed to enjoy going to school and he was well cared for but the truth was that he was losing his fight to lead a more independent life. There was no progress on toileting, communication, dressing, eating, behavior and the other IEP objectives, and we reluctantly, begrudgingly accepted the fact that it was time once again to adjust our expectations.

We had waged a fierce battle to make him normal. When that goal appeared out of reach, we set our sights on making him as independent and self-sufficient as possible. Finally, we capitulated to the grim reality that he would always be profoundly challenged, in need of intense care and support. Any small advancements would be gratefully accepted and acknowledged. We would cherish anything he could learn that would allow him to function better in a controlled work or residential setting. Our sights were now set on his long-term survival. Would he be able to function independently of us when we were no longer there to play our watchdog role? Could he minimize his dependence on others to meet his basic needs?

The Diagnosis Revisited

For sixteen years, we had labored under the assumption that Scott had cerebral palsy. This all turned on a dime when we read an article in the newspaper about the son of Dave Henderson, a professional baseball player who once played for the Boston Red Sox and Seattle Mariners. Mr. Henderson's son was diagnosed with Angelman syndrome, a neurogenetic disorder that was first discovered by English physician, Harry Angelman in 1965.

According to the Angelman Syndrome Foundation, Angelman Syndrome "shares symptoms and characteristics associated with other disorders including autism, cerebral palsy and Prader-Willi syndrome. Among the similarities were developmental delays, seizures, motor issues and lack of cooing, babbling or speech." Because of the similarity to other neurologic and genetic disorders, Angelman syndrome is frequently misdiagnosed, often for a long period of time. Since the similarities between Scott and Mr. Henderson's son were so startling, we felt compelled to learn more about this genetic disorder that occurs roughly in one out of twelve thousand to twenty thousand live births.

We pulled information from a variety of sources that led us to believe that there was a strong possibility Scott had Angelman syndrome. Today, this information is very neatly organized and catalogued within a variety of publications made available through the Angelman Syndrome Foundation. The following information was taken verbatim from the foundation's website.

Findings typically present in individuals with Angelman syndrome

- Normal prenatal and birth history, normal head circumference at birth and no major birth defects
- Normal metabolic and chemical laboratory profiles
- Structurally normal brain by MRI or CT
- Delayed attainment of developmental milestones without loss of skills
- Evidence of developmental delay by age six to twelve months, eventually classified as severe
- Speech impairment, with minimal or no use of words, receptive language skills and nonverbal communication skills higher than expressive language skills
- Movement or balance disorder, usually ataxia of gait and/or tremulous movement of the limbs
- Behavioral uniqueness, including any combination of frequent laughter/smiling, apparent happy demeanor, excitability, often with hand-flapping movements, hyper motoric behavior and short attention span

Findings in more than 80 percent of affected individuals:

- Delayed or disproportionately slow growth in head circumference, usually resulting in absolute or relative microcephaly by age two years
- Seizures, usually starting before age three years
- Abnormal EEG

Additional findings that Scott had in common with fewer than 80 percent of affected individuals

- Tongue thrusting
- Frequent drooling

- Excessive chewing/mouthing behaviors
- Uplifted, flexed arm position especially during ambulation
- Increased sensitivity to head
- Abnormal food-related behaviors

Scott had all of the symptoms shared by everyone with Angelman's and all of the symptoms shared by more than 80 percent of those diagnosed with Angelman syndrome. He also shared a significant number of symptoms exhibited by less than 80 percent of those with an official Angelman diagnosis.

Continuing to borrow liberally from the Angelman website, "in infants zero to twenty four months there was a lack of cooing or babbling, inability to support one's head or pull oneself up to a stand. The average child with AS walks between ages two and a half and six years and at that time may have a jerky, robot-like, stiff gate, with uplifted, flexed and pronated forearms, hyper motoric activity, excessive laughter, protruding tongue, drooling, absent speech and social-seeking behavior.

"Essentially all young children with AS have some component of hyperactivity. Infants and toddlers may have seemingly ceaseless activity, constantly keeping their hands or toys in their mouth and/or moving from object to object.

"Language impairment is severe. Appropriate use of even one or two words in a consistent manner is rare. Receptive language skills are always more advanced than expressive language skills. Most older children and adults with AS are able to communicate by pointing and using gestures and by using communication boards. Effective fluent language does not occur."

Well this certainly appeared to be one of those, "if it looks and sounds like a duck, it probably is a duck" situations. The symptoms seemed to fit Scott like a glove and went a long way toward explaining what we had been experiencing for over sixteen years. We decided to follow up immediately with the geneticist for Group Health Cooperative to see if she could confirm this diagnosis.

But, first, we needed to have a better understanding of Angelman syndrome. How did this rare disorder materialize in this tiny fraction of humanity? According to Genetics Home Reference, humans normally have forty six chromosomes in each cell, divided into twenty three pairs. Angelman syndrome is a malfunction of the fifteenth chromosome. Two copies of chromosome fifteen, one copy inherited from each parent, form one of the pairs. Chromosome fifteen spans more than 102 million DNA building blocks (base pairs) and represents more than three percent of the total DNA in cells.

"Angelman syndrome results from a loss of gene activity in a specific part of chromosome 15 in each cell. This region is located on the long (q) arm of the chromosome and is designated 15q11-q13. This region contains a gene called UBE3A that, when mutated or absent, likely causes the characteristic neurologic features of Angelman syndrome."

There are several genetic variations of Angelman's and a number of tests available to confirm the specific type of this disorder. Approximately ninety percent of Angelman people have their diagnosis confirmed with one of these blood tests. About ten percent test negative, but exhibit virtually all of the symptoms associated with Angelman syndrome. Of course that's just where Scott resides, in that purgatory of the clinically diagnosed. There was an additional test that could have been conducted at the time, but it was expensive and what real difference would it have made? It wasn't as though there was any cure or a treatment program available to treat the symptoms. At the time of his revised diagnosis, Angelman research was at a very embryonic stage and of relatively little value to Scott or his family.

The Group Health geneticist confirmed the obvious, that Scott shared all of the symptoms associated with Angelman syndrome. It didn't really matter whether his diagnosis could be confirmed with a blood test: he looked, acted and performed very similarly to other Angelman people. We even attended an annual conference of the Angelman Society and saw, for the very first time, a large number of children who looked and acted just like our son. Until that time, we thought he was alone in the universe. It was comforting and disheartening at the same time. It was nice to know that there were other people like Scott, fighting the same battles and struggling to find their place in the world. On the other hand, it was a final blow to our still- simmering hope that we could somehow discover a magic cure for his "brain injury."

Obviously, this was no injury to a specific region of the brain that could be dealt with through intensive, targeted intervention. We had been gradually letting go of this belief over the prior ten years, but it was still difficult to give up hope entirely. We were simply ambivalent about this new diagnosis. It was nice, finally, to learn that Scott had a tangible diagnosis, not this catch all cerebral palsy label. Cerebral palsy is used a little too liberally to describe anyone with movement disorders and it never really seemed to describe what we were observing with Scott. It was the easy place to locate Scott in the pantheon of disabilities, a lazy abdication. For sixteen years we were victims of a faulty diagnosis. We lost very valuable time that could have been used more productively to address his real disability.

It's not as though we received any direct help or assistance from local or national branches of United Cerebral Palsy. When he was first diagnosed, we sought out this organization asking if they could provide direct help or information. We were initially told that this organization focused almost exclusively on assisting adults with cerebral palsy. They gave us absolutely no source material and apparently they had no outreach program available to newly diagnosed families.

So, we were not prepared for the extraordinary competence and effectiveness of the Angelman Syndrome Foundation. In their words, the organization is there to "bring hope for therapies and ultimately a cure for AS. Angelman research also delivers hope to an even broader community of individuals because of the syndrome's connection to several other disorders, including Prader-Willi and autism."

One of the Foundation's principle strategies is to fund an array of scientific studies. To quote from their exceptional website, "most recently, ASF funding research conducted by Dr. Art Beaudet-prominent Angelman syndrome researcher at Baylor College of Medicine-continues to move closer towards potential clinical trials, a tremendous beacon of hope and promise for the Angelman syndrome community. Research is ongoing, but preclinical trials in mice have proven that symptoms of Angelman syndrome can be *reversed*, though more testing is needed to determine exactly how the cognitive deficits associated with Angelman syndrome are recovered.

"Previous ASF funded research has already proven successful in reducing the frequency and severity of seizures and research has confirmed that behavior intervention can improve neuro-developmental outcomes.

Further, "ASF funded research at the University of North Carolina-Chapel Hill, led by Dr. Ben Philpot and Dr. Mark Zylka, is making headway in learning more about the Angelman Syndrome gene, UBE3A and how it interacts with an FDA approved drug to potentially *reverse* symptoms."

This is really stunning news. When we first learned of this new diagnosis, we simply surrendered what little hope we retained for Scott's future development. We're now prepared to keep the pilot light on because the fire is not yet extinguished. There is, perhaps, a new dawn on the horizon. Hope is not dead and we need, for his sake, to maintain the course and wait patiently for reinforcements. Just possibly there is a way to win this prolonged and agonizing battle. Can you just imagine what this kind of breakthrough would mean for Scott? It would be like a rebirth, parole from a developmental prison. He would emerge into a parallel world, a world of possibilities and promise.

The Angelman Syndrome Foundation provides an impressive array of services and programs in addition to its' extraordinary scientific initiatives.

They have funded a number of Angelman medical clinics which provide a comprehensive array of services to Angelman families. The Foundation is in the process of expanding these clinics into a number of states throughout the country. Believe me, based on our medical experiences, this is extraordinarily important.

The Foundation also provides educational webinars, annual conferences, a family resource team and a parent inspired publication entitled Angelman A-Z. They are constantly experimenting with cutting- edge technology, like the IEP checklist I Phone application. They provide a veritable treasure trove of information on assistive technology, computer and software technology, education, employment, financing, inclusion, seizure therapies, and recreation resources.

Newly diagnosed Angelman families receive a level of support and information unimaginable thirty years ago. The marriage between technology and a very committed and formidable cadre of parents and advocates has given birth to an extraordinary support system. We tip our hats to this hearty group of pioneers and thank them for keeping hope alive.

The High School Years

Scott's remaining junior high school and high school years passed by uneventfully. We were approaching the dreaded advocacy burnout phase. We just didn't have much left in the tank. We couldn't keep pushing, pushing, and pushing without seeing substantive results. Perhaps it was time to give the poor kid a break and let him be himself, without the incessant prodding and poking. He had been on the front lines for the better part of eighteen years and he had fought the good fight. It was time to take our foot off the pedal and let him enjoy, to the best of his ability, his remaining school years. He had earned that right.

He was placed in supportive, nurturing special classrooms. His teachers and aides were caring and responsible. He was in the company of other special-needs kids who had very significant challenges. Whenever possible, he joined all of the regular students in the cafeteria, music classes or assemblies. He began to perform remedial chores around the school, like breaking down cardboard boxes. He began to ride his three-wheeled bike around the hallways. Some very wonderful students spent time with him on his IEP objectives and we became acclimated to the ebb and flow of special education. Call it capitulation, call it acceptance or call it wisdom. We had arrived at a different destination on his very special journey and it felt like the right place to be. Our interactions with both the junior and senior high schools at Lake Washington were unfailingly positive and we were satisfied that they were treating him with the respect he deserved.

When Scott was eighteen, we moved to Port Townsend, a bucolic little historic seaport on the northwestern tip of Washington State. I had just retired and we wanted a change of venue from the hectic lifestyle of the greater Seattle area. Our new home would need to meet certain basic criteria, such as being historic, artistic, beautiful and environmentally conscious. But most of all, it would need to be a progressive and welcoming place for the developmentally disabled.

Port Townsend seemed to fit the bill perfectly. A mutual friend with a developmentally disabled child had moved to this town recently and she raved about the quality of the special education program. She had just created a nonprofit called Gathering Place that was designed to provide recreational opportunities for the developmentally disabled. Additionally, another nonprofit organization, Skookum, had recently been created to provide innovative, sheltered workshop- style employment opportunities for developmentally disabled adults. They had created a jump- rope factory, a bakery and a recycling program for the developmentally disabled, remarkably progressive and exciting options for a town of 8,400 people.

This special town also had a number of adult family homes managed by a firm called Community Options that were significantly better than any homes we had visited in the Seattle area. This firm, under the caring direction of Leslie Sheinbaum, created very professional, nurturing home environments.

Port Townsend was also the seat of Jefferson County government. Jefferson County had a very progressive and caring developmental disability board that offered a wide range of services from parent coalitions to political advocacy. We felt very fortunate to have relocated to such an enlightened community.

We envisioned a transition experience for Scott in which the school would prepare him to work part time in one of the special employment programs. He would be able to take advantage of the special- recreation programs being developed in town and, eventually, move out of our home and into one of the adult family homes available through Community Options. A little euphoric perhaps, but not without a rational basis. We were just looking for a little stability, predictability and an accepting social environment.

Special- education students are permitted to stay in school until they are twenty one years of age. Scott spent the last two years at Port Townsend High School and we were pleased that he was treated well by his aids, teachers and fellow students. It was pretty much the same seg- regated special- education setting he had been used to at Eastlake High School. Everyone seemed to try their best to accomplish the various IEP goals, but he made very little visible progress, and he just drifted unevent- fully through his final years in the public school system. His time had come to a merciful end and the public schools washed their hands of any future responsibility. I hesitate to use the term accountability, because that concept never really came into play during his entire interaction with the public school system.

Basically, Scott was shown the door and wished the very best. He was now going to be home every hour of every day until it was time to leave his family for some kind of adult family home or institutional setting. It was a stark and unnerving transition, one that didn't reflect favorably on the public school system. His home away from home had just been permanently eliminated and we needed to replace this routine with something meaningful. No more bus to pick him up and take him home, no more school routine with teachers, aides and fellow students, no more IEP goals and objectives to pursue. Those six or seven hours out of the home for over half the calendar year were just eliminated for Scott and his family. It was just one long, permanent vacation from school, with the distinct feeling that nothing would ever come along to take its place in his life. He was shoved into social isolation and we were now compelled to create a new structure for his life.

It was a daunting task, one made infinitely more difficult by a complete lack of attention to this critical life transition. While we understand that considerably more attention is being paid today to this transition out of the public school system, fifteen years ago it was criminally neglected. There were no employment or day programs ready to replace the school experience. Scott was kicked to the curb unceremoniously, a victim of institutional apathy and incompetence. Suddenly, he went off the radar, a young man without a viable future or support outside of his immediate family.

His primary backup support was the Washington State Division of Developmental Disabilities. His caseworker prepared an individual assessment plan that detailed his specific needs and issues. The State becomes Scott's lifeline if and when Jean and I are no longer capable of performing our caregiving duties. They assign hours of support that he is eligible to receive for caregiving and respite services. The caseworkers and individual assessment plans will follow Scott for the remainder of his life.

The stable, predictable life that we've established for Scott in our home is, in many ways, illusory. It's only viable for as long as Jean and I are healthy and functioning at a reasonably optimal level. So far, Scott's caseworkers have been exemplary, but it's still a very scary proposition to have his long-term welfare in the hands of the State.

Transitions

This is as good a time as any to talk about the critical importance of transitions in the life of the developmentally disabled and their families. For most of Scott's life, transitions were handled badly by the various institutions involved with his care: hospitals, birth to three, primary school, secondary school, and post- graduation, employment and independent living programs. They invariably fumbled the handoff and we were left to sort out the ambiguity.

When the baton passed from one institution to another or from one division of an institution to another, it seemed as though we encountered one of those invisible electric fences. Once again, institutional self- interest triumphed over the needs of the developmentally disabled. They all erected their protective silos and showed relatively little interest in assuring a smooth transition. This occurs on both the sending and receiving ends of the continuum. With the single exception of the MESH program, we were never prepared for the next step. It was almost like a border crossing, where officials on one side of the border handed over the visitor to the other side. Passports were presented, responsibility was transferred and the individual was free to navigate his or her new environment.

Special attention needs to be paid to these transitions because they are pivotal to developmental progress. Regression always lurks behind the next bend in the road. Ineptitude and indifference can rear their ugly heads and wipe out months or years of developmental gains. Progress absolutely must be respected and reinforced as our person passes from one environment to another. Lip service simply doesn't cut it. Continuity should be the primary driver, not some stubborn institutional insistence on doing things the way it's always done them or introducing changes that sweep away years of progress.

Transitions have hurt Scott badly over the years. It's galling to us how little effort was put into creating seamless transitions. You don't just send a developmentally disabled person cold turkey from one environment to another. The physical space is different: the teachers are different: the students are different: the bus drivers are different: and the classroom structure is different. When our son made fragile gains in communication, toileting or behavior, we expected those who had been working with him to spend considerable time with those who would take their place in his life. It's only commonsense, yet it seemed as though we had to reinvent the wheel at every transition.

Part of the job for any person working on behalf of the developmentally disabled is to ensure that their person has every chance to succeed at the next stage in their life. You don't just close the institutional door and wish everyone the best of luck *until* you have completed this step. That is part of the job and to do less is simple negligence.

So after yet one more mismanaged transition, we were left to navigate uncharted waters. After all those years in early intervention programs and public schools, we were left with a twenty- one- year old adult/child who had no capacity whatsoever to meet his basic needs. He was still incontinent, unable to speak or communicate effectively, or dress, eat and bathe himself independently. He had impaired balance and very limited stamina. We still needed to shave him, cut his nails, change his DVDs, take him on daily outings, prepare all his meals, process his laundry and provide opportunities to exercise and recreate.

He had become extremely impatient, insistent on getting what he wanted immediately. Because he laughed so loud at things that amused him, it became impossible to take him to movies. Going out to eat at restaurants became a challenge because he would get loud and out of control if the food didn't appear instantaneously. He is also a very messy eater, so our choice of venues was fairly limited anyway. Due to his behavior issues, flying was no longer viable. Automobile vacations were now mandatory and the portable DVD player became our salvation. Yet, long car trips were not viable because of the difficulty he had in sleeping at strange motels.

Our lifestyle was governed by what he couldn't do and what he wanted to do. He still liked to ride his three- wheeled bike, go to fast food places, swim with his life ring at the local pool, go for walks in the grocery stores or big box retail outlets, play in the sand with cardboard boxes, watch television, look at colorful books and newspaper advertisements, color and play with beads. In other words, the caregiving challenge was twofold. First, we had to consistently meet his requirements of daily living. Second, we needed to accommodate his need to recreate and interact with his environment. Between these two mandates, we had relatively little time to focus and concentrate on other matters. We lived in a world of constant interruptions, an entire family afflicted with attention deficit disorder.

We had now graduated from interactions with the school system to interactions with the state and county DD delivery systems. The state caseworkers completed their individual assessments and we qualified for a certain number of personal care and respite hours. The county had a contract from the state to provide "community access": in which up to twenty hours a month could be allocated to getting Scott out into the community.

Caseworkers replaced school administrators, caregivers replaced teachers and the home replaced the school. We were sent out into wilderness without a first-aid kit, compass or survival gear. "We did what we could, sorry he didn't progress more, and please don't let that door hit you on the way out."

We started to cobble together a life after school. Initially, we took advantage of the twenty hour- per- month community- access program. This was one of those convoluted programs in which the state contracts with the county to provide a community outreach program. The county, in turn, contracts with various nonprofit organizations to deliver the program to eligible recipients.

So once a week, someone would come to the house and take Scott out to the swimming pool, park, grocery stores, ice-cream shop, beach or whatever else appealed to Scott. This was a very nice, though limited, break from the tedious and confining home routine. At the very least, it brought someone else into his life other than immediate family members. He could interact with a "buddy" and experience life outside the house. At least it struck a small blow against the oppressive isolation that permeated his life after school.

His community- access friends were, by and large, terrific, caring people. They enriched his life and he, in turn, enriched theirs. It made us feel that someone out there really cared about our son and that we could release our tight grip on him for a few precious hours. For the more profoundly disabled young adults like our son, this one-on- one community access program was a godsend. If anything, he could have benefitted from a more expansive access program, but, as usual, state budget constraints conspired against this option. Our very heartfelt thanks go out to Maury, Mary, Kathy and the other community- access professionals who came into our lives during these years. You are all very, very special people who make a great contribution to the most vulnerable among us. We know that Scott always viewed you as his personal friend. It brought us great joy to see how excited he was to see you and how anxious he was to leave with you on his next great adventure out of the house. You probably don't know to this very day what a great difference you made in his life.

Other than community-access, Scott had very few alternatives available to him at this time in his life. Due to his extensive physical, cognitive and behavioral limitations, he couldn't participate in Special Olympics, the weekly drop- in program at the community center or other programs that catered to the more developmentally advanced. At one time or another, we dutifully pursued all of these options, but they were just not feasible. This comment is not meant to denigrate any of these very important and worthwhile programs. They serve a critically important function for any number of developmentally disabled children and adults.

But for Scott, they did fit and his life was inexorably shrinking before our weary eyes. Was it possible that he had reached his developmental apex? Was there anything we could do to make his world more interesting, fulfilling and exciting? Did it even really matter to him? Were we stranded on an island, just the three of us struggling to make sense of a world that was passing us by?

Around this time, we were urged to invite a consultant to visit us in our home to map out a course of action for Scott. A number of people who knew Scott the best were asked to participate in an interesting exercise. Drawing paper was taped to all the walls and windows and we were told to illustrate Scott's life—his strengths, interests, limitations, hopes and dreams. We created a very unique visual depiction of his life, one that could be shared with anyone caring for him in the future. More importantly, we came to fully understand how important it was to bring more people into his life on a regular basis. He needed a "circle of friends" that could augment what we brought to his life. We were no longer enough, if we ever were. He needed a diversity of perspectives, experiences and personalities to enrich his life.

Caregivers

Only a life lived for others is a life worthwhile.

— EINSTEIN

We're private people by nature. We were not comfortable with opening our home up on a regular basis to strangers. It felt invasive and disorienting. Yet, it was time to open the floodgates and welcome personal caregivers and respite providers into our home to augment the community-access program. Scott needed other people in his life, and we needed a break from the routine and responsibility. The state, in its inimitable fashion, had its byzantine rules and regulations that governed respite care and personal care. For the most part, both of these services had to be conducted in the home, leaving us the option of sharing our space with strangers or hightailing it out of Dodge while they were in the house.

Caregivers are a unique breed of cat. The best ones are pure gold, irreplaceable and indispensable. The worst ones are your worst nightmare, indifferent, careless and irresponsible. The majority are somewhere in the middle, reasonably empathetic and willing to do basic assigned tasks. They don't see things to do on their own and made little effort to relate to us or Scott. We could be assured that our son would be safe, but anything beyond this level of care would be a bonus. They were there because they had to be, not because they want to be. It's a fundamental distinction, a bright line that separates the wheat from the chaff.

The people coming into our home are screened by the agencies contracted by the state to provide these services. But screening for criminal background is entirely different than screening for compatibility. We quickly learned that it's a hit or miss proposition. Their personal agendas, work ethic and personalities were all over the map and we were introduced to the concept of "match." Even though Scott's personal care plan was shared with the Agency and prospective caregivers and respite providers in advance, they often appeared tentative and overwhelmed. We went through some strange mating dance while we sized each other up to determine if we had a match. It's a strange dynamic. On the one hand, we didn't want to be rejected. On the other hand, we wanted to be assured that Scott was being cared for by a competent, caring person.

More often than not, we failed to find the appropriate balance. It's not too difficult to become a tad paranoid. We were rejected by some very weird personalities, leaving us scratching our heads in bewilderment. They might come for a day, appear to relate fine to Scott and us, and then inform their agency that they didn't want to return. At other times, they appeared to us to be a horrible fit, yet they stubbornly returned. At other times, Scott appeared to get along famously with the caregiver, yet we had absolutely no connection. We couldn't wait to leave the house when they show up, yet we still felt shoved out of our own home.

We started to develop better antennas and learned to differentiate the winners from the losers. We screened out the screwballs and warmly embraced the really competent, compatible and compassionate. We discarded our natural inclination to value privacy over all other considerations. For Scott's sake, we adapted and evolved as a family. It's been a valuable life lesson.

On those relatively rare occasions in which we achieved an ideal match, in which the caregiver, Scott and we were highly compatible, we were immensely relieved. We welcomed that person to our family, delighted that Scott had another special person in his life. When his most recent caregiver,

Trish, comes to the house, he runs out, gives her a big hug, takes her hand and insists that she immediately watch television with him. When we leave the house, he doesn't bat an eye and when we return, he couldn't be more content. This is such a blessing, to know that Scott is excited to see and be with another person, someone who brings an entirely different dimension to his life.

Just when we feel ready to throw up our hands and give up on finding appropriate matches, along comes an extraordinary person like Trish. Or Bobby, who, on his own initiative, took Scott to Seattle to watch the *Lion King* at the Fifth Avenue Theater. He also came to our house during a power outage when I was out of town and read books to Scott for a couple of hours. And there was Kathy, his aid at school, who would invite Scott to have dinner at her home with her family. These jewels were out there, ready to enter our life when we most needed them, when we were just about ready to give up on this idea of bringing people in to his life.

Although caregivers tend to be transitory, coming in and out of his life in an irregular, unpredictable manner, they are essential to allowing Scott to stay in his home for as long as possible. We are now in our seventies and challenged mentally, physically and emotionally to meet the exacting demands of caregiving twenty four hours a day, seven days a week. We need support and respite and Scott thrives on the different energy brought by the best caregivers. There is no place like a stable, loving home for a profoundly developmentally disabled adult and special caregivers provide the means to keep Scott home as long as possible. This is a special blessing and we are grateful for their compassionate support. They've extended and enhanced his quality of life, a gift of inestimable value.

Pathways to Employment

J ust as we were settling into a new routine of caregiving and community access, along came the newest state and county initiative to encourage "the least restrictive environment." Over the years, there were probably no people more supportive of programs that encouraged full inclusion and integration of the developmentally disabled than Jean and I. Whenever and wherever feasible, we strongly believe that the developmentally disabled should receive every opportunity to integrate seamlessly into society. There should not be artificial barriers erected based on labels, appearance or physical limitations. As stated previously, they should be given every opportunity to participate fully in whatever they choose to do in this world.

Unfortunately, the pendulum was swinging wildly and irrationally and Scott was wacked on the head one more time. Pathways to Employment was the newest rage and, come hell or high water, *everyone* was going to participate and benefit. In order to create individually designed employment programs for everyone under age sixty-two, established programs like community access and sheltered workshops would be phased out or drastically reduced. Workshops and training for unenlightened people such as ourselves were conducted to assure us that special jobs could be created for anyone, regardless of the degree of their developmental disability.

A tsunami was sweeping the DD world. Separate educational classrooms were being phased out in favor of inclusive programs; segregated, sheltered workshops were giving way to individual employment; state residential institutions and group homes were yielding to "least restrictive" residential options. People hanging on to the remnants of the antiquated, discredited programs were spitting into the wind. If some individuals were harmed by this new philosophy, well, progress demanded some sacrifices. "Pathway" zealots wouldn't concede that any of the prior programs had merit. They just stated emphatically that everyone would be far better off embracing the new philosophy, regardless of individual circumstances. Radical change required wholesale shifts in established practice and people just needed to get on board.

This was one of those times when we knew with absolute certainty that a program would not work for our son. We had come full circle. Where we once were firebrands, demanding innovative, progressive options, we were now perceived as reactionaries, jealously guarding the status quo. We had been transformed into the quaint older couple who had difficulty adjusting to change. We just didn't understand. If we kept our hearts and minds open, we would eventually come to appreciate this innovative program. Blah, blah, blah. Our concerns and protests over losing community access fell on deaf and arrogant ears. Particularly galling was the condescending reaction we received from a state consultant. Apparently, our personal, intimate knowledge of our son's capability was absolutely irrelevant, and he could assure us that *everyone* was employable. We just needed to stay open- minded, and we would eventually see the light.

The program just didn't make any sense for Scott. He was a victim of a philosophical shift that made no allowances for reasonable exceptions. This is what can be so maddening about well- meaning shifts in public policy. They can be intractable, bludgeoning precedent and proven practices. Incremental change is viewed as ineffective and wimpy, lacking in passion and commitment. Moderate, open- minded approaches are frowned upon. Yes, just like today's political environment.

The facts were abundantly obvious to us. First, Scott was participating in a community- access program that worked very well for him and his family. It didn't need to be replaced in favor of a theoretical employment program. Second, Scott was incontinent, with poor balance, stamina and cognitive capability. He had no reasonable means of communication. He didn't understand the concept of work and had no desire to engage in some simple, repetitive employment task. His behavior would go south as soon as he was asked to do anything that didn't make any sense to him. Third, there was no viable, economically productive employment option available to Scott, regardless of their insistence on finding some creative solution. Fourth, the only way this kind of program would work was if the job counselor literally did all of the work, while simultaneously riding herd on Scott. It was just nonsense, pure and simple.

Nevertheless, his community-access program was cut off and he was channeled into Pathways to Employment. We spent the next several years pretending to be in some type of individual employment program, aided and abetted by a job counselor. Since there was no earthly way a private sector employer was going to pay a wage to our son, they explored a variety of exotic options.

Two come to mind immediately. The first idea was to create a private business called Grounds for Perfection. Scott would collect discarded coffee grounds from various retail outlets, take them home to our garage, package them up in some acceptable form, and sell them at farmers markets. The high acidity in the coffee grounds presumably made them desirable plant supplements. If there was a demand for the product and he was paid money for his efforts, it would be up to his parents to keep the books, pay taxes and comply with legal requirements. The only problem with this idea was that the job coach would have to pick up the grounds, package them and sell them while simultaneously keeping an eye on Scott. Scott didn't have the fine motor skills, patience or cognitive capability to perform any of the required operations, but, my God, he would have a job! We finally nixed the idea before it was officially hatched, but we were very close to waking up one morning and declaring that "we were not in Kansas anymore."

After much soul searching, we settled on another approach. We would advertise in various local publications that Scott would be available to pick up people's laundry, take it to the dry cleaners, pick it up when completed and return it to the person's home. At least Scott could get out of the car, go to the door, meet the people, help bring the laundry back to the car and interact with the people at the dry cleaners. After a couple of months, we finally had one very kind lady give us a call and Scott had his first and only customer. The "business" failed, but everyone gave it the old college try.

Fresh out of employment ideas, it was decided that perhaps Scott should engage in a hybrid program that would bridge community access with Pathways to Employment. He would go out into the community much like he did with community access, but work on the prerequisites, like improved behavior, patience, physical stamina, and appropriate communication. Progress would be documented and eventually he would be in a better position to pursue job options. So that's where he was when the state finally sniffed the smelling salts and realized that, just perhaps, there should be exceptions granted for community access.

Scott went back on the community- access program, but not before irreparable damage had occurred. The employment fiasco had soured his interest in leaving the house with mercenaries who were hell- bent on grooming him for employment. The fun had gone out of the outings and he no longer left the house with the same kind of excitement and enthusiasm. We continued with the program for a couple more years, but it was clear that he had changed. His interest in the outside world had waned in the interim and his life began to shrink before our eyes. This was Pathways to Employment's lasting legacy.

Family Dynamics

The best way to find yourself is to lose yourself in the service of others.

— MAHATMA GANDHI

Perhaps it's time to digress a moment to discuss the impact a developmental disability has on the family dynamic. No matter how you rationalize, slice and dice and proclaim to the world that everything is perfectly normal, you are simply deceiving yourself. Things have changed and changed dramatically. It's of paramount importance that you gracefully accept this fact and make the necessary adjustments as a family unit.

This is particularly difficult as you try to help your person overcome the many obstacles placed in their path. You can't and shouldn't give up prematurely on his future. It's your job to see that he is given every conceivable opportunity to reach his God-given potential. This means that everyone in the family needs to be pushing harmoniously in the same direction. For instance, one parent can't be pushing aggressively for one therapeutic regimen, while the other gives up the ghost. One parent can't be fighting the good fight while the other gives up hope. Conversely, one parent can't be tilting windmills while the other is accepting reality and moving on to a more reasonable path. One parent can't behave boorishly, marching to his or her own drummer, leaving the burden and challenge to the other parent.

It's an incredibly complex dynamic. Somehow, someway, two parents need to confront a confounding developmental disability in a compatible fashion. They need to agree on what to do, when to make changes, who to believe and how to proceed. It's never static, so you have to make adjustments on the fly while still retaining your personal relationship. You need to retain a sense of humor and faith in the future even as you confront a never- ending series of disappointments and challenges.

You have to be able to accept defeat and still move forward together. You both need to accept roles that, perhaps, you had never envisioned. It's almost impossible to go through this experience without experiencing guilt, depression and, yes, rage. This means that you have to be there for your partner during his or her down times, pick up the slack and keep the family moving forward. You need to develop and sharpen your personal antennas, particularly if you are the partner working away from the home. The person dealing with the developmental disability daily, in all its manifestations, has, by far, the greater challenge. Although I felt the normal stress and pressure anyone does who has responsibility for bringing in the paycheck, it really paled in significance compared to what was happening on the front lines.

Your relationship is always in peril. You are both riding such an emotional roller coaster that it's a challenge to just be on the same page at the same time. Your child's developmental disability exacerbates the normal challenges that confront parents everywhere. Every issue seems to be magnified, demanding immediate attention and consensus. His future always seems to be hanging in the balance and we need to focus on his issues above all else. It's easy to lose sight of one another's needs and desires. This big elephant is always waiting in the closet, ready to break loose and trample your relationship. It's extraordinarily difficult to reach that magical equilibrium in which all members of the family receive enough time and energy.

A great many parents, for a wide variety of reasons, have to shelve their personal dreams and aspirations in order to raise a family. In that regard, we are no different from any other family. The fundamental difference is that we have to let go of the dreams we had for our child. Aside from missing the milestones referenced earlier, we also have to come to grips with the fact that our son will never graduate from school, marry, have children, pursue a career or chase his own dreams. He will always depend on others just to survive on a day- to -day basis. This stark reality keeps revisiting our conscience intermittently, leaving us vulnerable to depression and hopelessness. Our strong personal relationship, coupled with the sincere belief that he is living the life he was meant to live, guide us through the stormy times.

A certain liberation comes with this service- centered life. You learn to let go of closet aspirations and embrace the life you are allowed to live. It's all good, as they say. You learn to appreciate what you have and what you can do. You jettison that "grass is greener" attitude in favor of grateful acceptance of good health, loving family, good friends and a long, leisurely afternoon watching the Masters. There really is a lot to be thankful for and an amazing number of productive things we can do with our lives. There is just no point in belaboring that which is not available to you. It's a pointless and self-indulgent exercise, one guaranteed to blind you to all the possibilities still available to you.

It's certainly not shocking or surprising that a fairly high percentage of couples dealing with a developmental disability end up in divorce. Unfortunately, this usually means that the mother takes the day- to-day responsibility, often without the financial resources to cope. I have a very deep respect and appreciation for any single parent left with the responsibility of caring for a developmentally disabled child.

Siblings add another layer of complexity. In our case, our daughter is eighteen months younger than Scott and, by necessity, had to accept less attention than other kids her age. When you have someone in the house who requires the level of care and attention as Scott, something has to give with the other children. It's no small matter when someone needs to be within hearing or sight at all times. It's not a casual, unimportant thing. As a parent, you become conditioned to focus your energy and attention on the neediest child and you just hope that the other children can understand and accept this fact.

Our daughter, Stephanie, has always maintained that everything was just fine, that she simply didn't realize her life was that different from other children's. That's all she ever knew and she didn't harbor any resentment over any perceived slights or lack of attention. Although we made sure she had the full range of childhood experiences, from gymnastics, softball and horseback riding to playing in the school band, I often wonder if she was influenced, even subtly, by a special-needs brother who commanded so much of the family's focus.

She's always been very headstrong and determined to do things her own way, and we butted heads along the way. But she's evolved into a very strong, independent young woman, with a wonderful six- year- old son, Camden. She's an exemplary mother, probably a better parent than we were ourselves.

She's also chosen a giving profession, a decision that may have been influenced by her relationship with her brother. She works for a nonprofit organization providing help for drug-addicted mothers and their children. It seems to be a perfect fit for a strong woman who has had a front- row seat to the struggles of her developmentally disabled brother. She has a unique perspective that will be of inestimable value to young mothers facing their own demons.

Finally, extended family, for a wide variety of reasons, has not played a significant role in Scott's life. The immediate family has walked this unique fork in the road on its own, with relatively little involvement of other family members. Geography, generational differences, busy lives and our own reluctance to subject Scott to uncomfortable encounters have all contributed to this reality. Perhaps someday we can bridge this chasm, although Scott is less inclined these days to interact with anyone unfamiliar to him.

The Medical Paradox

Service to others is the rent you pay for your room here on earth.

— Muhammed Ali

As you could probably guess by now, Scott's medical and dental needs are unique and challenging. As he has aged, his health status has become a bit of an enigma. We can't tell, at times, whether he is getting the level of care and attention he needs at this time in his life. It really all depends on the degree of empathy and competence displayed by his primary care doctors and various specialists. We have to be diligent guardians, reminding physicians that it's time for home visits and blood draws. As he grows older and his physical and cognitive disabilities become more pronounced, we need to become more diligent advocates. It's all too easy to write off any and all medical concerns to manifestations of his disability. This problem or that problem just goes with the territory, not much can be done about it. In our opinion, that approach is a cop- out and various medical interventions should be available to treat his issues. He should be receiving, at the bare minimum, the same level of care and concern as anyone else.

He's not easy, we understand that. Doctors have to work harder at diagnosing his illnesses or medical conditions. He doesn't cooperate during the exams. In fact, he's terrified of going to the doctor's office and he raises such a ruckus that even they understand it's in everyone's best interest to visit him in our home. They have to exhibit patience, understanding and compassion. He's very strong and tactilely defensive. He makes it very difficult to take his blood pressure, weigh him on a scale, listen to his heart or examine his nose, ears or mouth. They have to really care and be willing to develop a personal relationship with a young man who doesn't understand why they are invading his personal space.

We've always worried incessantly about his physical health. He has no way of letting us know what part of his body hurts. He can't simply point to some body part to let us know where to concentrate our attention. Does he have an earache, stomachache, toothache or headache? Does the bunion on his toe hurt him when he walks? Is that why he can't seem to walk more than twenty or thirty yards at a time before stopping? What if he has tonsillitis, appendicitis or other life-threatening conditions that requires fast and effective treatment? What's happened to his balance and stamina? Why isn't he sleeping more than a couple of hours at a time? Why does he have these pronounced tremors of the hands and arms as he ages? How can we more effectively manage his weight gain? If his seizures appear under control, should we be weaning him off a lifetime of seizure medications? Is he possibly pre-diabetic? How do we know whether his eyesight is normal? He has to be nose to nose with the television, so it makes sense he could be dealing with a nearsighted condition.

These are valid concerns that need constant and diligent attention. His physical health is so ambiguous that it takes Sherlock Holmes-style physicians to investigate, research and solve problems on his behalf. It also requires health professionals who refuse to give up on him, who are willing to experiment, adjust and collaborate. They need to go the extra mile for him, giving him, perhaps, just a little bit more care and attention than they provide their "normal" patients.

The dental profession is an excellent example. We live in the northwest part of Washington State and have never been able to find a dentist to treat Scott. They just don't want to deal with the problems he presents, so he's denied access to dental care. Our saving grace has been the University of Washington's DECODE (Dental Education in Care of Persons with Disabilities) Clinic. We travel by ferry two and a half hours each way to have his annual exam and teeth cleaning. Very well trained and caring dentists and dental students staff this clinic. They treat the hardest cases with amazing grace and compassion. Although Scott needs to be strapped into a papoose board in order to restrain his arms and legs, they still treat him with care and respect. They are gentle, reassuring and professional---a real tribute to the medical profession.

At his last dental exam, we were informed that his teeth grinding is wearing down the enamel to the gum line. We are told that, given his cognitive problems, there is really nothing that can be done to deal with the problem. He won't be a candidate in the future for dentures or implants, so he will be relegated to consuming his food through a straw at some indeterminate date. Very uplifting news, but typical of the fatalistic forecast we receive on a regular basis from our friends in the medical community.

His medical care has always been hit or miss. We've had some amazingly caring medical professionals and some real clunkers. Like with every other profession, many practitioners are in that line of work for the wrong reasons. They just exude arrogance, impatience and indifference. Some clearly don't take the medical needs of the developmentally disabled very seriously. It can border on negligence at times, so we need to stay alert and demand competent assistance. On the other hand, we have a responsibility to let the world know when we are receiving a high quality of care. Scott is currently under the care of a very capable primary care doctor, a woman who genuinely cares and is willing to work hard on his behalf. This has not always been the case, so we don't take it for granted.

One example pretty much summarizes his lifelong love/hate affair with the medical establishment. We've been very troubled by his tremors. They are very pronounced and always present when he is awake and conscious. They have become worse with age, and we need to know what this means and what can be done to relieve the symptoms. Therefore, we contacted the University of Washington's Harborview Medical Center, which claims it does sophisticated research in this arena.

We made the requisite appointment two months in advance and waited patiently for the day to arrive when we could start getting answers to our questions. After waiting for over an hour in the aptly named waiting room, in came two neurologists who could have been auditioning for a part in *Saturday Night Live*. By this time, Scott was over the edge, hot, dehydrated, hungry, and soiled. These characters came waltzing in and let us know that we were kept waiting that long because they had to look up his condition on the Internet. Wasn't that just special? Apparently, two months advance notice wasn't sufficient, and they needed to take our time to get up to speed.

This bit of buffoonery was only surpassed by their brilliant diagnosis. Scott's tremors were probably as bad as they had ever been, but these medical wizards concluded that he didn't have any tremors. Apparently, they didn't mimic tremors exhibited by Parkinson's patients, so, by definition, he didn't have tremors. They didn't know what to make of the relentless movement in his arms and hands, but they were convinced they were not tremors. That was it: we were left with no diagnosis, direction, support or intelligent signs of life from Harborview.

On a positive note, the Angelman Foundation has been extraordinarily responsive to any and all inquiries we've made from our distant outpost on the northwest tip of the Olympic Peninsula. Their medical experts respond quickly and personally to all our questions and offer sensible and helpful advice. They are also on the right track with their plan to establish geographically dispersed Angelman clinics throughout the United States. This strategy will create one- stop shops for the full range of issues confronting Angels and parents and guardians will not need to continually rely upon uninformed medical people to address their various concerns. These clinics will also be on top of all the major research advancements related to Angelman syndrome and be bastions of hope and support. Given our personal history of haphazard medical care, this will be a welcome addition to our lives.

Random Acts of Kindness

No act of kindness, no matter how small, is ever wasted.

—AESOP

We would be remiss if we failed to take a moment to acknowledge those rare and special instances of genuine kindness. It's very, very easy to go to your natural default position and ignore Scott and his unusual behavior and appearance. It's always easiest to look the other way. This can be painful to watch at times, particularly for someone like Scott, who likes to make eye contact and reach out to people. He just craves validation and acceptance into the human family. We've had to continually restrain him over the years because he can be too aggressive and intimidating. It's obviously inappropriate for him to be grabbing and hugging strangers, family or friends and people naturally react by staying an arm's length away from his well- intended overtures. As we've always told everyone, he doesn't have a mean bone in his body, but we can't expect people to be clairvoyant. The constant indifference and rejection he experienced over the years has tended to make him withdraw from the majority of people he encounters. The exceptions to this rule are those who make a real effort to engage him and, of course, attractive women.

It's so very hard to understand and appreciate what life must be like from Scott's perspective. Can you imagine even going one complete day without saying a word? For most people I know, this would represent the end of the world. Compound the challenge by the inability to communicate your needs or desires through alternative means, like sign language, writing or picture symbols. It's a developmental prison, in which intimate thoughts, feelings and desires leak out inefficiently, inadequately expressed and inaccurately interpreted.

What if you couldn't let people know effectively whether you were too hot or too cold? Whether you had a craving for a certain drink or meal? Whether the sound was too loud on the TV or you were just not ready to go to bed? Whether you really needed to get out of the house and take a ride, or conversely, you just didn't feel like leaving the house to take a ride? Whether or not you wanted to go for a walk around the store, go swimming or go out to dinner? Whether you were scared of something? Whether you were sad? Whether you just needed to touch someone, have personal contact with another human being? Whether you couldn't stand the thought of being around a certain person for one more minute?

How must it be to never have a best friend, partner or lover? You are constantly exposed to the full gamut of human relationships on TV or videos, yet real intimacy is out of reach. All of your interactions with other human beings are closely observed and regulated. You want to express yourself in certain ways, but are always being restrained and rerouted. You want to laugh loudly at what you are see on television or a movie theater, but people constantly tell you to pipe down or leave the room. You want to connect with other people but lack the tools to interact normally. What if you could never have the kinds of conversations that we all take for granted every day? How was your day? What are we going to do today? Where do you want to go this weekend? What's for dinner? What did you think of your caregiver?

You want people to just leave you alone at times and stop cleaning your ears, brushing your teeth, cutting and combing your hair, giving you a bath, changing your clothes, cutting your nails and taking you for flu shots and dentist exams. You feel like you have little, if any, control over the most basic and intimate parts of your life. This makes you feel increasingly agitated and frustrated. Your unique view of the world is not something you can share with other people, so you can't really communicate whether you are feeling isolated and depressed. It becomes a guessing game for you and your caregivers. It's difficult to let people know whether you are generally happy and content or dealing with some kind of underlying despondency. You try to leave clues and bread crumbs, but the knuckleheads in charge are too dense to figure it out.

Everyone knows how it feels to be frustrated by complex technology. To Scott, the TV remote is a source of endless frustration. He doesn't know how to turn it on or off, switch to DVD, adjust the volume or change channels. Yet, he sees us do this for him and he grabs the remote, pushes all the buttons and screams bloody murder when the darn thing won't work right. He desperately wants to control his personal environment and he grows increasingly frustrated when everything seems out of his control. His tolerance and patience diminish with age. He has a harder time, as we all do, suffering fools. He knows what he wants, has a hard time communicating that need, and loses his temper when we are too slow on the draw or respond in an inappropriate way.

He does have his crude means of communication. He can whine, cry, scream, laugh, hug, kiss and physically demonstrate his needs. He can take your hand and guide you to the dining table. He can open the refrigerator and grab the jelly, reach into the basket and bring you a banana or retrieve a drink container. He can hand you the DVD he wants you to play next. He can come into our room in the middle of the night and grab your leg to let you know he needs the DVD changed. When you are walking in the store with him, he stops, grabs you around the waist and lets you know that he needs to rest. When he is full, he puts his spoon down and starts to get out of his chair. When he doesn't want to do something, like have his nails cut or mustache shaved, he physically resists.

This is how Scott copes with his world, one that is increasingly complex and baffling. And into his perplexing world come, on rare occasions, special people doing special things. They reach out to a vulnerable young man and offer something to make his life just a little richer. They don't expect thanks or recognition. That's not what makes them tick. They just see the chance to make a positive difference in the life of someone who doesn't have a lot of options or opportunities. We thank you for your humanity and compassion.

Quite frankly, these random acts of kindness are relatively rare. They are always unanticipated, generous and selfless. I've already cited a number of examples, such as people taking Scott to the theater in downtown Seattle, teaching him how to traverse the ski run at Snoqualmie Pass or taking him home to have dinner with the family. The entire staff at the University of Washington's DECODE medical clinic never cease to amaze me with their sensitivity and empathy. Many of Scott's volunteers, including my sister, are to be commended for traveling great distances and devoting personal time and effort to helping us with the home-therapy program.

Even small acts of kindness leave a deep impression. My friend, Jim Goodreau, dropped by our house in Port Townsend to temporarily store a kayak. While out on our front porch, I observed Scott in distress as he was coming back to the house from a walk with his caregiver. I had to go out and physically carry Scott back to the house because he had become exhausted. Jim called me the next week to let me know that he would be glad to drive two hours each way from Tacoma to help care for Scott and give us a break from caregiving. While we didn't take him up on his kind offer, we were always moved by the gesture.

A special thanks to Jasmine and Aladdin at Disneyland for breaking away from a line of kids to come over to Scott in his wheelchair and charm him with their good looks and great enthusiasm. The Mad Hatter walked by and told Scott not to let his parents push him around. Scott was thrilled with the attention of his Disney idols and I'm sure he has never forgotten this special time.

Christmas is Scott's favorite time of the year and Santa Claus is the star attraction. He hit the mother lode this year in Arizona. The Arrowhead Mall Santa actually got out of his chair, came out to the roped- off area and gave Scott a big hug and a candy cane. I thanked him for his great act of generosity, and he told me that special kids had a special place in his heart. It meant the world to Scott and it meant a great deal to his father.

Our Arizona neighbors, Don and Darlene Erickson, went above and beyond the call of duty when they came to our home dressed as Santa Claus and his helper. This was the only time in Scott's life that he was visited in his home by Santa Claus, and he was shocked and delighted. I have to tell you, it was a highlight film. He sat on the couch with Santa, opened the presents in Santa's bag and probably had the best Christmas moment of his life. You just can't overstate the importance of a gesture like this. It was a warm, fuzzy moment, one that comes into his life too infrequently.

A very sincere and heartfelt shout-out to our one- time neighbors, Dave and Sherry Ellis. They have never, in thirty- four years, forgotten Scott's birthday or Christmas. He always receives a card and a present and it has been over thirty years since we were neighbors. They are affectionately known as Aunt Sherry and Uncle Dave and they have assumed an important place in his life. He was never forgotten and always validated. Thanks for always being there, during good times and bad.

Neighbors came to the rescue several times in our Tuscany neighborhood in Redmond, Washington. Once, during an unanticipated and unprecedented snowstorm, neither Jean nor I could get home to get the kids off the school bus. I was so panicked that I ran ten miles in the storm in my work clothes after my car stalled in a snowbank. Our neighbor, Judy Heitloff, intercepted the kids, made them a hot drink and cared for them until we could eventually make it home. We were enormously relieved and grateful. On another occasion, we couldn't locate Scott after he went out to play in the dirt and another neighbor helped scour the neighborhood until we finally located him in someone's home. Quite honestly, you get to the point where you don't think anyone else could or would care for or about your disabled child in an emergency. It was nice to be proven wrong.

Though these kind overtures have been relatively rare over the past thirty- four years, they, nevertheless, have restored our faith in humanity. They also stand in stark contrast to the phony sainthood bestowed on various teachers, aides, caregivers and others who make a living working with the developmentally disabled. Some certainly deserve the praise and admiration they receive, but far more just care about making a dollar

There is probably nothing that annoys me more. First, this misplaced adoration discredits the value of the developmentally disabled person.

Second, it assumes the person providing the care receives little, if any, return, financially or emotionally, for their contribution. Third, it has a chilling effect on oversight and performance. Some folks think these good-hearted people shouldn't be held to high performance standards because they selflessly devote their personal and professional lives to the developmentally disabled.

We most admire and respect those people who quietly and immodestly offer love, support and acceptance to our challenged son. They do these things for the right reasons. They don't expect thanks, acknowledgment, compensation or payback. They are special people offering a helping hand to a special young man.

These gestures are also very personal and intimate. They stand in stark contrast to the lightning- quick change in communication technology and the impact this is having on social interactions. Information technology has a tendency to de-emphasize one- on- one interaction in favor of more dispassionate and anonymous communication. While technological advancements can and do offer important support to the developmentally disabled, they need to be viewed in context.

What Scott wants and needs is nothing more than more people willing to spend time with him, caring about him, taking him out to lunch, going for a walk or watching a movie. He wants people to interact with him on a human scale, with a laugh, smile and conversational banter. This is the polar opposite of Twitter, Facebook, texting and all the other multitasking technology that has become so ubiquitous. So while society is inexorably losing its capacity to develop strong, personal, intimate relationships, Scotts' needs remain old school. He likes eye contact, human touch, cuddling and laughter. He responds to genuine, empathic and sunny dispositions. He is a human barometer, capable of ferretting out the disingenuous, indifferent, and uncaring.

He is the antidote to the frantic, dog- eat- dog, pace that is systematically devouring and dehumanizing society. He requires a society that values compassion, sharing, serving, loving and sacrifice. His long- term survival depends on unconditional love. More importantly, mankind's long-term survival requires a course change in this same direction.

The Long-Term Question

No one is useless who lightens the burden of another

— CHARLES DICKENS

As we all age, the big question looms over our head: where will Scott live and who will take care of him when we are can no longer do so? This is the question that haunts parents of developmentally disabled children and adults everywhere. When do we finally let go and trust that others will love and care for him as we have done his entire life? Over the years, we have read one horror story after another about caregivers of profoundly developmentally disabled adults abusing and neglecting them at both institutional and residential settings. Our loved ones are exceptionally vulnerable to the capricious and depraved acts of sociopaths and con artists. Sexual, physical and emotional abuse are always a risk for the non-verbal, cognitively challenged DD adult. Even if these more egregious acts are absent, neglect and indifference are always lurking right around the corner. How do we find a place where Scott is respected and loved? A place that will really get to know him, care about him and assure his long- term health and happiness? When do we reach that point where it is in Scott's best interest, as opposed to our own, to place him in another residential setting?

This will probably be the most critical transition in his life, one that we are reluctant to initiate. Many friends, acquaintances and professionals have advised us for years to make this change sooner rather than later.

Their reasoning goes that Scott needs time to adjust to new surroundings while we are still around to guide and oversee the change. We are getting older and more vulnerable to a wide array of physical ailments and conditions, making it increasingly likely that a harsh and unanticipated residential placement could be on the horizon. If this should be the case, then it's quite possible that Scott will be placed in whatever opening is available, one that might be totally incompatible with his needs and personality.

Clearly, we don't want Scott to be warehoused in an institutional setting, one that will effectively remove him from society. This is a chilling prospect, one that would make him invisible and inconsequential. He would gradually recede into an institutional purgatory, one lacking in genuine love and affection. His unique personality and individuality could be smothered, snuffed out by indifference and abuse. At least that's what we fear the most about his future.

Many more -enlightened residential options have surfaced over the past thirty years or so. Due to intensive lobbying efforts from DD advocates, the vast majority of developmentally disabled adults are now being placed in "least restrictive" residential settings. For those on the higher rungs of the developmental ladder, this means they have their own apartments, with targeted caregiving assistance. They receive help with personal finances, medical needs, transportation, job training and other requirements of daily living.

DD adults such as Scott, who cling to the lower rungs of the ladder, need significantly more help to remain in a viable residential neighborhood. A variety of residential models have evolved over the years to meet this mushrooming demand. A substantial number of adult family homes have been created that house six or fewer residents and are managed by for- profit or nonprofit organizations. They are licensed by the state and financed by a combination of sources, from social security payments, Section Eight housing vouchers and Medicaid personal care to contributions from family members.

Long- term residential care is a bit confounding, from both an emotional and financial perspective. For some fifteen years, since Scott was first ushered out of the public school system, we constantly requested information about how to plan for his eventual relocation. It was yet one more example of how poorly the DD system handles critical transitions. All we were asking for was a roadmap, some clarity about how this part of the system worked, how it was financed and how much lead time would be necessary to achieve a comfortable, humane transition.

The first thing caseworkers always told us was that the state provided very limited funding to accommodate all of the housing requests. There was always some kind of mysterious slush fund that seemed to materialize to handle genuine, critical emergencies, but we couldn't count on its availability to achieve some kind of orderly housing transition. This meant that, should something traumatic happen to either Jean or myself, the state would step in and place Scott in whatever residential slot was available. Whether or not it was an optimum, or even suitable, response to Scott's needs and personality was immaterial. He would go to whatever was available, end of story.

Well, this delightful situation creates a dilemma, a regular DD puzzle. If we keep Scott in our home indefinitely, it's the equivalent of walking a tight rope without a net. He will probably never receive the same level of love and care he receives in our home, so it's only natural that we would want to keep him in his safe and comfortable enclave for as long as possible. If we gamble too long on this strategy and he needs to be transitioned immediately, the change could be too harsh and unforgiving. He might be placed in a cold, sterile, abusive environment, one that might be a living nightmare.

The problem is compounded by a lack of funding and planning. It would cost approximately $300 a day, or around $10,000 a month to pay for an alternative residential placement. Since he receives a fraction of this amount from Social Security, Medicare and state respite support, he would need a major increase in funding to accomplish the goal. To bridge this funding gap, Scott would need to receive what the state calls a Core waiver. This designation would provide the necessary funding for Scott to receive the full range of support he would need in an alternative residential setting.

Doing the rational thing, we apply, year after year, for a Core waiver. The request is routinely denied, usually without any explanation whatsoever. We are told we can appeal the ruling, but on what basis? We don't even know why his request was denied, our very own catch- 22. So if we can't get the Core waiver, how can we have a serious conversation about alternative placement?

This is frustrating to us for a number of reasons. First, since adopting Scott almost thirty- five years ago, we have saved the state a minimum of $3 million dollars in caregiving expense. If any family should be in line for additional financial support, it would be ours. Yet, we constantly see younger, less disabled adults placed in intensive support homes, simply because their families are no longer willing or able to provide for them in their own homes. The state plays this strange game of chicken with families such as ours. They virtually dare us to declare an emergency and scream "no mas," When the family persuades them that the crisis is real, they swoop in and take the child to the most suitable placement option.

We understand both the problem and the strategy. There is not enough money in the system to accommodate the huge backlog for residential placement. This prevents them from working with families to plan for gradual and rational transitions from the home to the community. They set aside just enough funding to handle the emergencies they know will occur in any given funding cycle. This results in a clumsy, awkward response to a very predictable need, creating anxiety and confusion for families of the developmentally disabled adults.

Of course, the root problem can be traced back to a reluctance on the part of the electorate and elected officials to provide the necessary tax support. Despite the heroic and often effective lobbying efforts of DD advocates, the spigot has been slowed to a trickle. The political system has become paralyzed, immobilized by partisanship and irrationality. It's always been a struggle for DD advocates to secure funding for a broad array of educational, medical, dental, employment and residential needs. They have been tireless, impassioned and well informed, but it's never been easy.

In theory, it should be a slam dunk. The primary role of government should be to provide for the public good and protect its most vulnerable citizens. For a brief, enlightened period of time, both Republicans and Democrats shared this perspective. Democrats typically wanted to extend tax support to a wide array of needs and causes, and Republicans believed one of the few legitimate purposes of taxation was to protect society's most fragile and vulnerable. It's a measure of any just society. It's a staple of all major religions. It's a moral imperative, one that should automatically override most other claims for the tax dollar.

DD advocates have been very successful over the past several decades because of their tenacity and absolute commitment to a righteous cause. But they are beginning to get major pushback from ideological zealots, folks who have drawn a line in the sand on any new taxation. The public realm is under assault and the developmentally disabled are collateral damage. A political tidal wave has been sweeping across the nation, one that has the potential to sweep away decades of progress for the developmentally disabled.

It's become a hostile, uncompromising political battlefield. Rational, reasonable initiatives don't even see the light of day. DD advocates are in scramble mode, forced to protect existing funding levels and defend critical programs. Despite huge increases in DD caseloads and requests for services, there is simply not the political will and leadership to deal with the problem.

Older parents like us who care for developmentally disabled adults lack the energy to be both a caregiver and political advocate. Perhaps at a younger age we could take on both jobs, but now it's a virtual impossibility. So we must rely on the good work of advocacy organizations like the Association for Retarded Citizens to carry the banner on our behalf. We weigh in whenever possible with phone calls, candidate meetings and e- mails, but the bulk of our energy must be directed to caring for our son.

Despite the best efforts of a great many fine people, there is still not enough money in the system to meet the long term housing needs of all those who need to transition out of the home. The number of families who would like to place their adult DD person outside the home far outnumber the number of slots available. So the State Division of Developmental Disabilities has had little choice but to routinely deny Core waiver requests, unless there is an eminent and compelling reason to do otherwise.

This reality has inspired many families of developmentally disabled children and adults to create nonprofit residences. Groups of families purchase homes, pool resources, hire staff and manage homes with minimal state oversight and involvement. These alternative solutions are increasing in popularity, but they require significant investment in time, energy and resources. It's a burden that the families of the developmentally disabled shouldn't have to bear, but it is becoming more the norm than the exception. This is particularly true for younger families.

As we enter our seventies and Scott begins to regress, our caseworkers have begun to work more closely with us on identifying viable long- range housing options. They make it clear that when we are finally ready to make the transition, they will do what's necessary to secure the Core waiver and get Scott placed in an acceptable home. They sensitively leave the decision and timing to us. It's still not the type of orderly, rational transition that we would prefer, but at least we no longer feel that we are left dangling off a cliff.

Over the years, we have visited a number of adult family homes, hoping to find inspiring, nurturing living environments. For the most part, we were discouraged and disappointed. Most were sterile, impersonal places, staffed by people who would rather be anywhere else in the world other than where they were. They were located in marginal neighborhoods, poorly maintained and without any sense of warmth and hominess. They felt like an institution outside the institution, poor substitutes for a genuine homes. They were actually scary places where we wouldn't dream of relocating Scott. We were deflated, convinced that Scott would have very tough sledding when the time finally arrived to move him from his loving home.

A very pleasant exception to these experiences was a tour that we were given of adult family homes managed by Leslie Sheinbaum in Port Townsend, Washington. Her firm, Community Options, contracted with the state to provide residential services to developmentally disabled adults. Without exception, all of her residences were well managed and had the feel of real homes, replete with warm décor and loving staff. It was a great relief to know that such places actually existed, that Scott might someday have a place to live that could accommodate his unique needs and personality.

Leslie demanded a high level of performance and she worked hard at hiring and training a first rate staff. Her homes took on her personality and were reflecting her values and commitment to the developmentally disabled. They had a personal, human touch, very rare and much coveted by all families of DD persons. Unfortunately, Leslie sold her business to a national corporate entity not too long ago and the jury's still out on whether her legacy will endure.

Although funding for residential placement continues to be erratic and unpredictable, we are reasonably convinced that the combination of our advanced age and Scott's very high degree of need will conspire to get him the coveted Core waiver. This is certainly not a sure thing and we could be left waiting at the altar if and when we decide it's time to make this agonizing decision. We would much prefer a more rational planning approach that would give us more time and information. We need sufficient lead time to visit alternative homes, interact with staff and management and reach a reasonable conclusion.

In recent years, our caseworkers have been exceptionally thoughtful and supportive. If anything, they are encouraging us to make this monumental decision and begin the process of requesting a permanent residential placement. I suppose they have concluded that we've paid our dues and that it's probably in the interests of Scott, the state and ourselves to make this transition as painless as possible. Because of the unpredictable nature of state funding, there is always the possibility that the necessary financial support might not be available if we procrastinate too long.

Once we make the decision to proceed, we must be prepared to move quickly. It will, to a large degree, be a huge leap of faith. How much do we really trust the long-term care system for the developmentally disabled? Will the home be located in a good area? Will his caregivers attempt to provide an interesting and fulfilling life for him? Will they tolerate all his quirky habits and behaviors? Will they show restraint and patience when he gets too demanding at meal time or in the car? Will they take him to McDonalds or the mall or Target to make sure he gets out of the house, exercises and interacts with people?

Will staff be a good match for Scott? How will he relate to these new people? Will they take good care of him, and meet his extensive personal care needs with care and dignity? Will they change him regularly, keep him clean, process his prodigious laundry, brush his teeth each night, keep his nails trimmed, shave him and bath him? Will they get up at night to switch DVDs, or give him a drink of milk? Will they tolerate his temper tantrums when he doesn't get fed quickly enough? In short, will he be genuinely loved, cared for, and respected? Will he be safe?

I suppose that both Jean and I have concluded over the last fifteen years following Scott's "graduation" from the public school system that he will never have the quality of life somewhere else that he has in our home. He's comfortable, happy and loved. We understand him intimately, willing to do whatever we need to do to make his life happy and fulfilling. We're joined at the hip, forever entangled. While our attention was diverted, someone emptied our bucket list. We're not dying to unload a part of ourselves in order to pursue unfulfilled dreams. Somewhere along the way, all those things that seemed so important at a younger age, began to seem irrelevant and a bit superfluous. After all, it was Scott who was dealt the short straw. Despite all that he can't do and all that he can't be, he still manages to make the most of a very bad hand.

So we are not going to make this critical placement decision based on any other criteria other than what is in Scott's near- and long- term interest. It's a Hobson's choice. If we move too precipitously, we could be denying Scott his last, best years. If we accept the premise that he will never have it as good as he does right now, then why would we move up the timetable? He's in a loving, happy place, a place that's familiar, secure and comfortable. As he regresses with age, he needs an even greater level of support. Why not ride this elevator down with him as long as possible and make the change when we are left with no alternative? Our conscience would be clear. Our job would be done and Scott would be in God's loving hands.

On the other hand, if something happens to any one of us as we hover above the snapping alligators, Scott would be subjected to a potentially brutal transition. We would all be emotionally unprepared to handle this radical transformation. Quite possibly, we would be in no position to oversee the placement or monitor his care. This means that he could be placed in a home all too similar to those we found so abhorrent. Wouldn't this be fundamentally irresponsible, a benign neglect that would place Scott in peril?

Obviously, this decision weighs heavily on us as we all age and battle our respective ailments and infirmities. We're reminded daily of our acute vulnerability. We can't be content with assuming the ostrich position, pulling our head out of the sand only when someone pokes us in the posterior. As for now, we are trying to balance the two perspectives. We will continue to do the necessary research, visiting prospective homes and preparing ourselves to make the move when the time is right. It's perhaps our last critically important decision to make on Scott's behalf. We just hope and pray that we're given the wisdom to make the right one.

The Long Good Night

If you light a lamp for somebody, it also brightens your path

— BUDDHA

The autumn of our lives has passed and winter is squarely in our headlights. The three of us are getting a sneak preview of the final chapter. As our energy, stamina, and resilience surrender to the merciless demands of aging, Scott undergoes his own transformation. If we live long enough, most of our lives move in a circular fashion, from total dependence on others to total reliance on others. In the intervening years, we experience what life has to offer and leave our imprint on the world. Hopefully, we've left a legacy of accomplishment and contributed in some meaningful way to making this a better place. Scott, with all his limitations, has done exactly that. He's shared his love, laughter and spirit with his family, caregivers, classmates, teachers, bus drivers and everyone else who came under his spell. He's special in the true meaning of the word, one of those rare souls unencumbered by the nonsense that characterizes most of our lives.

It hasn't been a cakewalk for Scott or his family. This isn't a story about overcoming all the obstacles and achieving amazing results. We are not trying to wow you with the spectacular success story, claiming that his developmental disability was no obstacle to achieving his life's dreams. If anything, Scott's story gives the lie to the tired adage that you can overcome anything through hard work, dedication, inspiration and faith. Despite herculean efforts to "fix" the disability, his genetic aberration trumped all the well-meaning intervention strategies. He is still profoundly disabled thirty- four years later, his normal life derailed by a rogue gene that insidiously alters all aspects of daily living.

When you begin as far behind the starting line as Scott did, you have an entirely different definition of success. I doubt whether Scott even had any dreams or aspirations. If he did, he had no real way to communicate those to anyone who could offer a helping hand.

But this is precisely why we felt compelled to tell his story. The vast majority of developmentally disabled adults live life well outside the radar, just like the rest of us. They crave acceptance and understanding and want to live life to the fullest. They want you to know that their lives matter, that they are full-fledged members of the human family. To be sure, Scott's challenges are as significant as they come, but they don't diminish his worth or value. He's changed the world in his inimitable way, perhaps more profoundly than most of us. Each of these special people contribute something very important to the world and don't need to be validated by showcasing some unique attribute or talent.

Scott is mirroring the life cycle experienced by most of us, but he's doing so at an accelerated pace. His "circle" just has a smaller circumference. He's experienced infancy, childhood, adolescence, early adulthood and, now middle age. He's been curious about his world, living life with vigor and enthusiasm. His limitations have, by necessity, restricted his exploration of the world. He's only been able to do a fraction of what the rest of us have done, but he's still done so with a genuine love of life.

He's beginning to struggle. Life has become more difficult and challenging. He can no longer walk independently for more than a few yards. His balance is precarious and he is constantly at risk for falling. His stamina has diminished dramatically. While he use to walk for blocks and swim in his life ring for hours, he no longer has that capability. He's lucky to walk from his bedroom to the dining room and even this small distance requires physical assistance from one of us. Because we think it's important for him to get out of his bed or couch and get some exercise, we try to take him out to the grocery store or big-box retail outlet at least once every other day. Although he still has the desire to go to the store and look at other people and exercise his legs, he still needs to stop and put his arms around me every couple of minutes.

He's lost interest in many of the things he used to love. He doesn't like to read the Sunday- morning ads, take baths, go swimming, ride his three -wheeled bike, play with beads, color, chew gum, take walks in the neighborhood, play with cardboard in the sand or many of the other things that interested him over the years. These interests have evaporated and have been replaced primarily by television and eating. His world is shrinking, as it does for most of us as we age. Nevertheless, it's hard to watch.

He's gained quite a bit of weight and doesn't sleep for more than a couple hours at a time. He's developed a voracious appetite, one that has to be monitored and restrained. Since he took a spill and nearly bit off half his tongue, he has developed an exasperating habit of sticking both hands in his mouth for a good part of the day. He's drooling more and his eating has become very messy. His patience has diminished, and he has a short fuse when he becomes hungry or wants a DVD replaced.

Our lives revolve around his eating and sleeping schedule. Much as with a newborn, our sleep is constantly interrupted by his loud, frequent demands for a DVD change, food, or drink. His circadian rhythm has been completely and permanently distorted, so our sleep patterns have altered accordingly. We are perpetually sleep deprived. No matter what we try, it doesn't work. Leaving the TV on, turning it off, giving him sleep medication, discouraging daily naps, changing nighttime temperatures- you name it. And, please, don't ask medical professionals for any help, because they don't have a clue.

He wants to have his morning meal at four thirty or five and his lunch around eleven and his dinner at four thirty. His internal clock is infallible, so there is hell to pay if we fail to stay on schedule. For someone who can't tell time, speak or communicate in any meaningful way, it's absolutely amazing how he keeps us in line.

He loves to go out to eat, but we need to go to the right establishments. They have to have the right kind of food, be "family" friendly and be amenable to serving a messy and, at times, loud customer. We've learned to eat out early, before the restaurant becomes too busy. Over the past couple of years, Scott has become more insecure and he needs to cling to me like an octopus throughout the meal. We've gotten to the point where we feed him anything that he can't get in a large spoon or eat with his hands. I suppose it's a bit of a spectacle, but most patrons and servers are discreet and respectful.

We've also learned to order quickly and precisely, with a special request to bring milk and bread out immediately and his main order out before ours. The timing of the meal is of paramount importance. If it comes out too late, he has a tantrum and we are both frustrated and embarrassed. We have identified a number of restaurants that fit our bill of particulars very well, with good food, outstanding service and a good overall environment. Our personal thanks and compliments to those owners and servers who have shown such great sensitivity and understanding over all these years. It's meant a lot, giving us a taste of normal in our decidedly abnormal life.

As Scott changed over the years, we've had to make many adjustments, both large and small. As previously mentioned, we can no longer go to movies, fly on airplanes, or eat out at quiet, upscale restaurants. On car trips, it really helps to have a DVD player on the back headrest. We live in perpetual fear of power outages. He goes ballistic without television or DVD shows, so we need to have backup portable DVD players available that can get us through six to twelve hours of a power outage. In fact, we will probably need to invest in a backup generator to ensure that we can survive a significant power disruption.

We have not had the option of attending family functions with Scott for a very long time. For whatever reason, he seems to panic in unfamiliar surroundings and demands to leave immediately. We spent so much time attending to him that we didn't have the opportunity to interact with family members. It was so stressful and demanding that we just quit going to anyone else's home. He's generally very good about staying in his room when we have company over to our house, so this becomes our only real social option. On rare occasions, we get caregiving help for a longer time period that allows us to attend a special occasion like a family reunion, wedding or neighborhood gatherings.

Because of all this change and disruptions, to our daily lives, we've come to embrace flexibility. Our lives demand sacrifice, but we are rewarded by love and a strong sense of purpose. Scott has allowed us to lead a purpose-driven life, one that places a premium on love, service and faith. He shares his special spirit with us. It's an irreplaceable gift. Priorities are rearranged and we understand that we are placed on this earth to make a difference. It's clearly not about who has the most toys, or has seen most of the world, or has the greatest number of experiences or has amassed the most power and influence. It's really about love, service and connection to a higher authority.

We enter this last stage of our life with our eyes wide open. Change is occurring rapidly and we know that Scott will need to be cared for by others before too long. We've all had a good run, doing our very best under the circumstances.

Kubler-Ross developed a grief model many years ago that included denial, anger, bargaining, depression and acceptance. Usually, people experience significant loss and move through these cycles with some degree of predictability. For those of us caring for a developmentally disabled person, this process never seems to come to any kind of closure. Acceptance keeps getting deferred as we deal with the diagnosis, promising medical developments, breakthrough treatment regimens and our own determination to defeat and overcome the developmental disability. Our grief keeps reemerging with each new setback, making it challenging just to keep our heads above water. Expectations are constantly recalibrated and the grieving never quite leaves our consciousness. We learn to deal with it and, eventually, we reach an enlightened stage characterized by complete acceptance. Our loved one is just fine and we are lucky to be in his loving embrace.

Whatever Scott has had to endure, he's done so with grace and acceptance. We wake up most mornings to his belly laughs. His world, like those of many people his age, is shaped by virtual reality. He loves and identifies with a variety of television and movie characters. He gravitates toward happy, upbeat movies, ones that are full of laughter and music. His peer group, from his perspective, are all those incredibly talented young people who star in *Glee*. He loves almost all musicals, comedies, and Disney productions. He disdains violent and angry productions.

He brings joy and happiness to those lucky enough to be part of his world. He should not be defined and perceived by his limitations. He adds value to the world through his profound influence on those who intersect with him in a meaningful way. Whatever we've had to sacrifice on his behalf has been paid back in full. He's one of God's ambassadors and we are privileged to have played a role in his life.

If you want happiness for an hour, take a nap: if you want happiness for a day, go fishing: if you want happiness for a year, inherit a fortune: if you want happiness for a lifetime, help somebody.

—Chinese proverb

Lessons from An Angel

Lesson #1- Parents are the child's best advocate. Don't give up on your child for any reason at any time. Parents know their child better than anyone else, care more than anyone else and are more committed than anyone else. Be receptive to innovation and inspiration, but retain a healthy skepticism.

Lesson #2- Manage the pendulum swings. Parents of developmentally disabled children are fair game for zealots and snake- oil salesmen. We tend to look for quick fixes from dogmatic and arrogant messiahs. Keep striving and experimenting, but do so rationally and deliberately. Climb on the shoulders of those who came before you and learn from their accumulated wisdom and experience. Place a premium on research, science and evidence-based approaches.

Lesson #3- Find fellow travelers to share information, hope, experience, fears, failures and successes. You can't travel this path alone for long without falling into despair, grief and hopelessness. There is, indeed, strength in numbers and you will find role models, fellow advocates and lifelong friends. It's an indispensable part of coping with a developmental disability.

Lesson #4- Proactively engage with family and friends. Don't lock them out or let them off the hook. Your child needs the support and understanding of extended family. You just hurt yourself and your child over the long haul when you curl up in a protective shell and go it alone. It's hard, painful and emotionally draining, but you need to do whatever you can to create a strong, family support system for your vulnerable child. Ultimately, a closer relationship is good for both the child and extended family.

Lesson #5- Parenting a child with a developmental disability requires tenacity and a bulldog determination to take on all challenges. You have to stick your chin out and run interference for your child when that becomes necessary. Timidity and equivocation will get you nowhere. You are fighting a righteous battle for the most vulnerable among us and that should get you through a lot of tough times.

Lesson #6- The human spirit is transcendent and indestructible. Your developmentally disabled charge is probably more spiritually advanced than the vast majority of people on the planet. You've been blessed.

While you are at it, lose the preoccupation with whether your offspring reflects favorably on you in terms of appearance, behavior and accomplishments. No, you don't have a mini-me to carry on the family name and put impressive notches on the family tree. What you do have is a special, one- of- a kind, human being whom you will love unconditionally. Your soul will be retrieved, gift wrapped and returned intact.

LESSON #7- Personal happiness and freedom are reflections of the choices available in our lives. Our loved ones should receive a full range of choices to meet their needs and desires. Developmentally disabled persons should be able to choose how they want to live, work, recreate, attend school and interact with other people. It's imperative that we recognize this fundamental right, whether it's being challenged by an ignorant public, regressive policy makers or overzealous DD advocates focused a bit too much on one branch of the DD community.

LESSON #8- Share your story. It will humanize your child, give his or her life greater meaning, and help with political advocacy and funding. Play your part, champion the cause and demand to be heard by decision makers. Be visible, loud and compelling. Shame those closed- minded ideologues who would starve government, no matter what the cost to those who can't help themselves. Republicans and Democrats share an historical empathy with the developmentally disabled. Exploit this rare confluence of opinion by making your needs well known. The developmentally disabled should always be a priority for the endangered tax dollar. A just and honorable society takes care of its most vulnerable citizens.

LESSON #9- Don't assign sainthood status to everyone working with your child. Stop acting like a puppy dog wagging your tail every time some professional spends time with your child. This warps your perception and fails to hold "experts" responsible and accountable. Professionals, whether in education, employment, medicine, housing or caregiving are like professionals everywhere, some are good, some mediocre and some horrible. Learn to make the distinction and resist the temptation to be indiscriminately grateful for any attention paid to your child. Time is always precious when you are trying to climb that developmental ladder and the last thing you need is to be derailed by incompetent, indifferent and condescending "experts." And, by all means, praise and reward the genuinely empathetic and capable. They are few and far between, so, please, spread the word that someone out there is making a difference.

LESSON #10- With Individualized Education Programs (IEP), learn to differentiate between form and substance. Special education was forced on the vast majority of local school districts across the United States and rigorous reporting requirements accompanied this legal mandate. Our experience with special education was that the school administration was focused on complying with legal requirements, not teaching and learning. As long as they could check off all the boxes, they were perfectly happy. They would hold individual education meetings with parents, outline goals and objectives and be relatively unconcerned if your child failed to meet any of his targets. As long as they followed the process religiously, results and accountability were unimportant. This is ass backwards. You should demand flexibility, creativity, results and accountability. *It's not always your child's fault.*

LESSON #11- The special education hierarchy can be totally asymmetrical. Those on the lowest rungs, with the least pay, credentials and status, have the greatest influence over your child's educational progress. Those at the top are preoccupied with legal, political and administrative issues. Ironically, at the annual IEP meetings, all the air time is taken up by those who are least familiar with your child—the various specialists, principal and special education administrators. Be prepared to work closely with those most important to your child's development, the classroom teacher and personal aids. Simultaneously, be ready to do battle with the guardians of the bureaucracy because they will be focus on the needs of the institution, not those of your child.

LESSON #12- Transitions are crucial. You need to spend an inordinate amount of time and attention on these pivotal moments in your child's life. You need to make sure he or she has a soft and manageable landing. Those folks who are passing the baton need to familiarize those on the receiving end. Your child shouldn't enter the transition cold turkey. That's simply a prescription for disaster. Frankly, it's inexcusable and all too common. So when your child moves from a birth- to-three center to elementary school, from elementary school to junior high school, from junior high school to high school, from high school to employment or community access, and from home to community living, everyone should work overtime to make sure the transition is smooth and painless. It's the logical, humane thing to do.

LESSON #13- All people have inestimable value, regardless of the degree of their developmental disability. Their influence radiates through those who love and care for them and those who come in contact with them on a regular basis. They make those around them better people. They inspire and motivate those closest to them to become more productive, empathetic and resilient. The developmentally disabled contribute to society in a great many ways and they should be respected and embraced. Genetic testing needs to be conducted in an ethical context instead of being used as a vehicle for eliminating an entire branch of humanity. Scientific advances should be directed at curing and helping, not at exterminating the outliers.

LESSON #14- Maintain balance in your life. It's too easy to spend a disproportionate amount of time on the person with the developmental disability at the expense of work, health, friends and family. This, in turn, will do great harm to the very person to whom you are devoting so much time and attention. The last thing he or she needs is for family relationships to fray or jobs to be lost or family members to become mentally or physically ill. Stability is essential to the well-being of your loved one and you owe it to him/her to take care of yourself and the rest of the family. The rest of the family also counts and should receive the appropriate amount of love and attention.

LESSON #15- Demand attention and accountability from the medical profession. Don't let these "helping" professionals be dismissive, unconcerned or irresponsible. Make them work! Seek answers and expect some flexibility and ingenuity. Don't be passive spectators when it comes to the health and well -being of your loved one. You need to be their voice and private medical investigator. Don't shy away from becoming a loud, persistent advocate, particularly as your person ages and medical issues become more significant.

Truly, I say to you, as you did it for one of the least of my brothers, you did it for me.

— Jesus

Living with and caring for a person with a developmental disability is not for the faint of heart. It's also not a walk in the park for the developmentally disabled person. The challenges are enormous, but the payoff is also extraordinary. You discover a parallel world, a world full of love, compassion and insight. We wouldn't have traded this life experience for any other. This extraordinary young man has never said a single word to us in thirty-four years. But his love is transcendent, an overwhelming presence in our lives. He knows he's loved. He knows how proud we are of him. He knows that he's an irreplaceable member of our family. He's found his place in the universe.

This concludes the story of Scott's first thirty- four years. It's been an extraordinary journey! God bless Scott and all of his developmentally disabled brothers and sisters. You've made all of us better people, and you've made the world a better place!

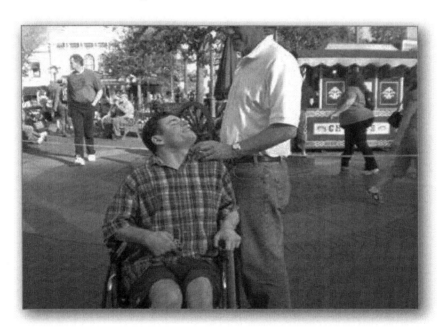

Made in the USA
San Bernardino, CA
06 July 2015